If Keynes Were Alive Today. . . ?

THE U.S.A. IN THE WORLD ECONOMY

Eminent Economists, in Interviews with Professor Arnold Heertje of
Amsterdam, Discuss for Us the Problems of the Decade

FREEMAN, COOPER & COMPANY
San Francisco, CA 94133

337.73
U 58

Acknowledgments

We acknowledge gratefully the cooperation of all those who have made this English edition possible: Among them Meulenhoff Informatief of Amsterdam; the ten scholars who were interviewed; Alan Blinder for his "postscript" and its original publisher the *New York Times;* Robert Ishi for his imaginative help on the design; and the translator of Professor Tinbergen's article, Yolanda van Ecke-Klot.

10-9-8-7-6-5-4-3-2-1

Printed in the United States of America
Library of Congress Catalogue Card Number 84-081000
ISBN 0-87735-801-X
　　0-87735-802-8

CONTENTS

FOREWORD

During the summer of 1983, I interviewed ten economists of world fame. These interviews were broadcast by the Dutch radio station AVRO that fall. They are contained in this book, with a concluding essay by Professor Alan S. Blinder.

Some of the economists I spoke with have received the Nobel Prize in Economics; others may be potential candidates. All the conversations were based on one initial question: "What is your perspective on the world economy in the eighties?" The answers show a wide variety of arguments, visions, and even emotions, but there is always a consistent framework of economic analysis.

I shall not attempt to distinguish rigorously among the economists interviewed but an overall grouping of their answers may prove helpful. Some think in terms of a supply-side model, others emphasize the importance of demand factors, and one adheres to the monetarist approach. Supply-siders have a tendency to relate stagnation to the troubles with which the private sector is confronted, such as the heavy burden of the public sector and high labor costs. Demand-oriented economists relate stagnation to lack of effective demand on the part of consumers and producers and to the decline in world trade. Monetarists explain the high level of unemployment and the pessimistic attitude by price inflation, in its turn caused by too much money in circulation.

These three visions of economic reality provide us with three scenarios for economic policy. A policy rooted in "supply-side" economics tries to create more room for the private sector and entrepreneurial activity in order to stimulate private investment and, therefore, growth and employment. A Keynesian "demand-side" policy seeks to stimulate public expenditure in order to improve economic conditions in the private sector. The question of how to finance such an expansionary policy often remains unexplored. A monetarist policy aims at a reduction in the growth of the money supply by the Central Bank. Monetarists assume that this will bring down the rate of inflation and the rate of interest and will lead to economic recovery. Most monetarists deem this restricted monetary policy not only necessary but also sufficient.

The following table summarizes the opinions of the economists represented here in terms of the catchwords *supply-side*, *demand-side*, and *monetarism:*

	Supply side	Demand side	Monetarism
A. K. Sen	X	X	
M. Bruno	X	.	
L. R. Klein	X	X	
M. Friedman			X
J. K. Galbraith		X	
R. L. Heilbroner	X	X	
J. Tobin		X	
F. Hahn	X	X	
J. M. Letiche	X	X	
J. Tinbergen		X	

Reading this book is a simple and effective way to obtain insight into current views of the possibility of a world recovery, its probable strength and perseverance, and the conditions that have to be fulfilled in order to avoid another period of stagnation and massive unemployment. I am very happy indeed that American readers, too, will now have this access to the opinions of these leading economists. In this respect, I would like to express my gratitude to Professor John M. Letiche for his advice and help in accomplishing this goal.

IF KEYNES WERE ALIVE TODAY ...?

Professor Amartya Kamar Sen was born in Santiniketan, India, in 1933. He is currently "Drummond Professor of Political Economy" at Oxford, England. He completed most of his studies in economics in England; he attended Trinity College at Cambridge, where he received his Doctorate in 1959. He is an honorary member of several academic organizations. He lectured at a number of American universities as a visiting professor. He gave seminars in numerous countries on diverse economic topics.

Professor Sen focuses on the theory of growth, especially as it relates to problems of developing countries, and on the theory of collective decision making. He is regarded as an eminent theoretician.

AN INTERVIEW WITH
AMARTYA SEN

OXFORD

Professor Heertje: *We would like to discuss certain aspects of your views about the development of the world economy, not only this year but more in particular during the coming years, let's say during the eighties. Perhaps you could give your global view about what you think will happen in the economic sphere.*

Professor Sen: Well, I fear I can't make great predictions about what will happen in the rest of the eighties. However, I should be surprised if the present depression (what we have *is* a depression, I think, rather than just a recession) would very easily lift completely. My guess is that there will be quite a few false starts, and the depression—especially high unemployment—will continue for another few years. And when all this comes to an end and there is another powerful boom (as undoubtedly there will be eventually, in the usual pattern in which the world economy moves), I don't think we shall find that we have resolved many of the older long-run problems that had caused difficulties earlier.

But are you expecting that we are coming back to more employment or even full employment?

Yes, I think in a few years time, the employment level will rise. Not because of the effects of the present economic policies. I think the

11

present economic policies, say, in Britain and in America, will not, on their own, lead to substantial economic expansion. But the general cyclical pattern of booms and slumps still operates. Further, we must take into account the political dimension too. I think the high level of unemployment is already appearing to be quite intolerable in most countries. It has not yet had a very strong impact in Britain, because of the fact that the Labour Party has not yet been able to convince the electorate that it has a viable and well-thought-out alternative. (It may or may not be a mistake to think that the Labour Party doesn't have a viable alternative, but that has clearly been the common belief.) So the pressure on the government is not yet strong, but I would expect it to become much stronger in a few years time. In fact, I would expect this to be happening throughout the Western world— in America and in Western Europe, and much stronger pressure for a more fully employed economy will build up. And I think that must lead to a political change of policy—more towards expansion and less concentrated exclusively on avoiding inflation. And when that happens, and the employment level does rise, I would expect all the older problems to reappear. I don't see that any big institutional change has taken place.

So, you would think that it would start all again? Over-capacity, over-expansion, budget where the government having huge deficits again, etc.?

Well, I don't know whether it will exactly take that form, but—yes— there will be many similarities with the past. I think the main dif-ficulty is this. There are strong needs for having a pattern of eco-nomic expansion based on cooperation between different sectors and different groups. Essentially, planned coordination of some kind. However, what we really have is a cyclical behaviour: when the employment level is very high, the unions are very powerful, and they can call the tune; when the employment level is very low, they can be pushed around and battered. We go through a kind of cyclical pattern on that. Now if, instead of that, we had more of a cooperative kind of economic expansion, then some of the problems might not have occurred. But it is not easy to see that happening—at least in Britain or in America. The government's reading of the situation seems to be that by unilateral action on the part of the government (plus reliance on free enterprise), it is possible to achieve a situation of high growth, low inflation, high employment. But I don't see any evidence that this is likely to happen.

You don't think that the recent experience in the United States, with monetarism, trying to tighten credit and to raise the rate of interest in order to cure inflation, that that didn't point in that direction, I mean?

I don't think so. For two reasons. Monetary policy does, of course, have the "advantage," from the point of view of the government, that it can be carried out unilaterally. You can carry it out even without any agreement with the unions, without any kind of coordinated planning; you don't even need the backing of legislatures or Parliament, as you do for raising taxes. So from this point of view monetary policy is a "marvellous" instrument. The government can simply change monetary controls—they don't need new legislation, they don't need anything. Any political set-up that tries to rely on free enterprise, on the one hand, and a powerful conservative government, on the other, is bound to regard monetary policy to be an attractive instrument of control, because you can avoid the need for "cooperation"—cooperation between different sectors of the economy and different groups and different classes. So that's one reason for its appeal. The other reason of course is that given enough time, it can affect the employment level (by cutting it quite severely), and through that the rate of inflation too. Now, we have got no evidence really of any country which has been able to cut down the rate of inflation through monetary means without at the same time cutting down the level of employment quite severely. This need not worry the government too much if the nature of government policy is not based on working with—and for—all the different classes and groups, but is a unilateral policy carried out with a highly sectarian outlook. If there is unemployment, people simply "will have" to take the consequences of that. While it is quite effective eventually, the process is not even terribly fast; in the countries with such policies, high inflation survived for many years. In this country, in Britain, it is only relatively recently that inflation fell. After the conservatives came to power, for quite some time the inflation rates were very high indeed—higher than under the previous government. But eventually through a clamp-down on the economy, it did have the effect of reducing inflation. But it is a very expensive way of achieving the result, especially because of unemployment and wastage. One might ask, why incur such a lot of expense, why sacrifice so much output, so much growth, so much employment, and why cause so much social misery? What for? And I think the only advantage of it is that this is one policy which the government can carry out *unilaterally*, without needing anybody else's consent.

They would argue perhaps that the perspective of long-run growth and an improvement of the long-run employment situation would be helped by following a policy like that as they have done in the recent years.

Yes, but I don't know on what empirical evidence that argument would be based. There is little empirical basis for concluding that having high unemployment, combined with low inflation, is particularly good for economic growth. Now, it is certainly true that starting from a position of high unemployment with a reduction in unemployment you can have what looks like "growth." We are seeing this in Britain currently. Once employment level expands, it looks like a big jump of growth rate. But that is of course just absorbing a part of the slack in the economy. This is like the high growth rate after the depression of the 1930's. But if one thinks of sustained, long run growth rates as such, these growth rates typically have not been very high in periods of low demand and restrictive public policy.

But don't you think there is some kind of a recovery at the moment, and that it has something to do with the policies followed in the United States?

The interesting point about the recovery is not that it is occurring now, but why it is so late. One expected recovery many years ago. Most governments, actually, went on predicting upturns. Mrs. Thatcher's government had been predicting recovery quite a few years ago. When a number of economists teaching in British universities wrote a letter, a few years ago, saying that the policy should be changed because the country was going into a depression, we were all laughed out of court. And there were statements by economists in the government and by other experts arguing that in fact recovery was already taking place. In fact, since recessions and depressions are followed by recovery, it was not unnatural to expect a recovery. But something delayed the recovery. Now, after many years, despite the delay, there may well be some signs of recovery. But even now the signs are not very clear. Even if we assume the most favourable scenario, namely, a full-fledged recovery now, that would not, of course, indicate that the recovery is due to government policy—in particular the policy of curing inflation through restrictive monetary policy. I think it is just that if you have a boom-slump sequence, you would expect a recovery to take place. The depression was longer than usual; the bottom levels that we reached in terms of decline of output, decline of employment, etc., were in most cases more severe and more lasting than had been expected. If there is a little bit of recovery now, the defenders of government policy can't really take credit for a "successful" economic strategy.

So, you would be inclined to argue that there is a recovery more or less independent of the economic policies that have been carried through?

Yes, I would say that government policy hasn't helped much. Of course, the government could have followed *even more* of a restrictive policy, even higher interest rate, and could have cut down on the money supply even more strongly, making recovery that much more difficult. But it is one thing to say that the government *did not entirely stifle* the recovery, and it is quite another to say that they have *ushered in* a recovery through their own policies. No, I would certainly dispute that.

I see. One other question in this respect, about technology and the influence of technology on the unemployment situation. Would you think that the severeness of the unemployment problem is strengthened by new technologies in the application of. . . .

Well, I think that's a very complex case. I think the short answer to that is yes. The new technologies have had the impact of replacing a fair amount of labour, so that when expansion takes place, the output expansion is not matched by employment expansion. But I think there's a longer answer, namely, that it is possible to deal with the problem of technological transformation in a way that does not make the employment situation so bad. And I think that is again a matter of planning, which I was mentioning earlier. I think it is a question of having a much more clear-cut and conscious policy about dealing with the technological issue in the Western economies, and to see how sensibly one can use the benefit of better, newer technology, which after all has the beneficial effect of reducing drudgery, reducing the hardness of work, giving people more leisure. The question is how to combine that with giving people the things they want (including work). Guaranteeing incomes, satisfactory jobs, good circumstances of work, etc., and permitting people to cultivate their capabilities as much as possible, require much more of conscious planning than the Western economies have typically been inclined to do in recent years.

Could you think of, I'm sure you can, of other areas where you could concentrate on for the coming years. I'm thinking in particular of the relationship with the third world.

Yes, I think that's an important question too. The third world countries represent a political force that is not terribly powerful, and therefore the circumstances of the third world countries have not really affected the policy in the richer countries very much. The recession or depression, of which we were talking earlier, has had really disastrous effects on the third world countries, and this is sometimes overlooked. One of the things I have tried to argue in my last-but-one book, *Poverty and Famines*, is that quite a few of the larger famines have taken place at a time when the food situation, in terms of availability per head, had not been particularly bad. In fact, they have taken place in situations of good food availability, judged in terms of food output, or food supply, per person. They have taken place because some groups of people, some occupational groups, some parts of a class, have suddenly lost the basis of their earning an income. It could be rural labourers losing jobs because of, say, floods in Bangladesh in 1974. Or it could be the Sahelian or Ethiopian pastoralist nomads losing the opportunity of selling their animal products to buy food grains at a cheap price in order to survive. These changes could bring about a famine. One of the results of the depression in the Western world (and indeed also in the socialist countries, to some extent) has been to hit various occupation groups in the poor countries very hard—those who rely on exporting goods to the richer countries. And these groups have suffered tremendously. Quite often they actually suffered acute hunger through this period, due to the recession in the West. Guaranteeing employment, income and the means of livelihood can be done through public policy. When people say in the West, that we ought to have more austerity, cutting down on employment and cutting down on output, etc., they overlook that this would imply austerity not only for themselves, but also for the rest of the world (including many of the poorest countries in the world). Sometimes forcing the additional "austerity" on people who are least able to bear it. One of the issues that is bound to come up, in this context, is that of the relationship between the richer and poorer countries. Also those *among* the richer countries themselves and *among* the poor countries. There is a good case for extending the *intra*national coordination to *inter*national cooperation.

So, summing up, you are not too optimistic about the recovery? You think that if there is some kind of a recovery we will come across more or less the same kind of problems we have had in the past, about inflation, about governments being in difficulty which increases everywhere, and also the problems with respect to the third world, you would still think that they are still there and very severe?

Yes, what I am saying is that (i) if the recovery takes place now, which is by no means clear, and (ii) if it is strong, but (iii) if all this occurs without any substantial institutional change in the cooperative direction, we would be back precisely where we were. We have to think about the totality of the economic systems, and how to change them. We have to re-examine the relationship between the different countries, and the relationship within a country between workers (and unions) on the one hand, and the government, the employers and other groups. We have to think also about social security arrangements. Some people have argued that social security arrangements strongly affect incentives; there have been fruitful debates on that subject. But no matter what the incentive effects are, social security is the means through which hunger has been prevented in these countries. Otherwise, with the level of unemployment that we have in Britain today there would have been severe and straightforward hunger in this country. It hasn't happened because of social security. This is not to deny that social security also may create incentive problems. But to deal with these diverse problems requires more conscious cooperation between the government and the public, and between different groups, and a more conscious pursuit of economic expansion, rather than relying on the magic wand of monetary control or some other simple formula.

I understand you're also saying that we are not rid of the unemployment problem by just saying that we have the possibility to provide for social security because the problems for the unemployed are much more severe than just to be cured only by social security.

Yes, exactly. I would, of course, also say that social security has indeed reduced substantially the *harshness* of unemployment. There is no question that that is so. But you're absolutely right. One can't view the problem of unemployment just as one of guaranteeing incomes, if necessary through social security. It is a defeatist's way of looking at the problem; ultimately people also like being involved in production and having jobs, and they want to be employed. Fruitful employment is one of the fundamental needs of human beings. And it is also the means of producing output and having a prosperous economy.

Okay, well, thank you very much.

Thank you.

In conclusion:

Professor Sen is quite concerned about the lack of institutional change, which could prevent a recurrence of inflation and an overheating of the economy. He fears a repetition of patterns from the past, with strikes, over-ambitious wage demands from unions and stagnation of growth. He sees the need for a bargaining model for the primary economic groups, which could result in some planning and coordination for the most important economic activities.

Professor Michael Bruno was born in Hamburg, in 1932, emigrating to Israel in 1933. Professor Bruno studied mathematics at Hebrew University in Jerusalem and at King's College, Cambridge. Afterwards he studied economics in England, Israel, and the United States. He has been Professor of Economics at Hebrew University in Jerusalem since 1970.

His scientific contributions up to now have been in the area of growth, and capital, theory. His research has been theoretical as well as empirical. He was, for example, involved in the so-called Cambridge controversy, a debate on the fundamentals of economics, which lasted through the sixties and seventies.

AN INTERVIEW WITH
MICHAEL BRUNO

JERUSALEM

Professor Heertje: *I would be interested in how you regard the economic prospects for the 1980's.*

Professor Bruno: I learnt a long time ago that it's very hard to make predictions about the future. Suppose you had interviewed various economists at the end of the sixties as to what the prospects were for the 1970's. I'm sure that, like the OECD at that time and the various national financial institutions, all of us would have projected a decade of continued rapid growth, with some fluctuation in inflation rates—a very different world from the one we actually faced. I would therefore like to start by talking about the problems of the past decade. My main reason for hesitancy about the prospects for the eighties comes from the fact that I'm not sure that we've really solved those problems.

In the past ten years we've had a much slower rate of growth and a slowdown in productivity in all industrial countries, we've had inflation rates that were both higher than before and fluctuating much more, and we've had rising unemployment. When we come to ask ourselves why this has happened, there are a number of theories. I happen to believe that the shocks the world system has suffered in the past ten years have been different to those sustained earlier. In the 1950's and the 1960's, fluctuations in economic activity usually resulted from changes on the demand side—namely, booms with full employment and inflation, followed by recessions in which demand contracted, either of its own accord or because of conscious government policy. As a result we had business cycles in which high unemployment was followed by periods of full employment with inflation.

In the 1970's, the most marked change was the phenomenon of stagflation—accelerating unemployment together with inflation. And this leads one to think that the trouble was more on the supply side of the macro-economy. And when I say the supply side, what I have in mind are shocks to the system resulting mainly from the prices of factors of production. We had major oil price shocks in 1973 and 1974, and another one in 1979–80. We've also seen rises in real wages, another type of supply factor. In the past two years, moreover, we've experienced a different kind of price shock—the rise in real interest rates. Even though the world seems to be starting on a period of recovery at present, with inflation rates and nominal interest rates having come down, real interest rates are still very high. In fact, they're much higher than they've been for the past fifteen years. I would consider that a supply side shock too.

How are all these things connected? At the end of the 1960's and the beginning of the 1970's, the Bretton Woods system of exchange rates, which had existed since the end of the Second World War, collapsed. This, as we all know, was caused by monetary factors— the huge outflow of dollars from the United States during the war in Vietnam and Cambodia. The breakdown of the exchange rate system introduced fluctuations into the world system that may partly be the reason—not the only reason but partly the reason—for the fluctuations in relative prices.

The oil price increases of 1973–74 were certainly an independent factor. They were not caused by exchange rate policy. But raw material price fluctuations in the early seventies—the fast rise in 1973–74, followed by a fall and then another rise—were partly connected with political forces and movements in relative exchange rates.

The response of a typical industrial economy to a raw materials price increase or an oil price increase is a rise in unemployment and a rise in prices. Profits fall and producers seek to produce less and raise their prices. They also cut back on their investments. In the seventies, because of balance of payments problems and inflation problems, sometimes wrongly perceived, governments by and large chose the course of cutting down on domestic demand. So you had a Keynesian anti-inflation policy that caused Keynesian unemployment on top of the type of unemployment, not known in the fifties and sixties, that in Keynes's day would probably have been called classical unemployment, resulting from the fact that real wages were too high relative to the kind of real wage level that would adjust the labor market.

That was a new phenomenon, which manifested itself both after the first oil shock and after the oil shock in 1979–80. Now if you ask how one can account for the fact that real interest rates have risen in the past two years, well, that comes partly from the anti-inflation policy followed by the United States and willy-nilly by the other industrial countries because of exchange rate fluctuations that would otherwise have been much worse. There was a real interest rate squeeze after the second oil shock that we didn't have after the first oil shock.

You say the rise in real interest rates results partly from U.S. monetary policy. What about other reasons?

Well, it's not something that I'm 100 percent sure about, but after the first oil shock there was a drop in real interest rates in world markets that had a very interesting side-effect on the world economy. It seems to have been very different after the second oil shock. Now, why did real interest rates come down the first time around? My way of accounting for it—and this has been proposed by other economists as well—is by looking at the real interest rate determination in world markets as resulting from a combination of what happens to world savings and world investments. This is now a much more integrated capital market than it ever was before 1973. The way to account for the drop in real interest rates is by looking at what has happened in the recycling of petro dollars. As a result of the rise in oil prices, you had a massive accumulation of foreign exchange in the hands of the OPEC countries, which had to be recycled into the world financial system. Since one country's deficit is the rest of the world's surplus, someone had to pick up the OPEC surplus. Surprisingly enough, the industrial countries did not follow a deficit policy after 1973–74. As a result of contractionary domestic policies, they on the whole balanced their current accounts. The balance of payments deficits occurred in the Third World—in the middle-income industrializing countries, which borrowed very heavily on this newly formed private capital market. But reluctance on part of the large oil users to pick up the OPEC surplus brought down real interest rates. Real investment demand came down more than savings, and that has pushed down interest rates.

Now after the second oil shock, the industrial countries remained in deficit for a more prolonged period, partly because of large fiscal budget deficits. There was thus greater competition for the OPEC surplus, and this raised real interest rates. That may be a more important cause of high interest rates than the monetary squeeze. After all, a monetary squeeze accounts for a rise in nominal interest rates, but it cannot explain long-term high real interest rates—unless inflationary expectations are really way off.

So you don't think high budget deficits, particularly in the United States, are responsible?

No, I think they are. I think they are. The crowding out effect on interest rates is at least as important in accounting for the high real interest rates as the monetary squeeze. It's a macro-system and you have to look at both monetary and fiscal effects. Unless we understand it fully, it's very hard to make predictions about the chances of real interest rates coming down, for instance. And lower real interest rates are an important factor in world recovery.

The last point that I'd like to touch on in looking at the past, before we return to your main topic, is labor markets—namely, behavior of real wages. Why should a raw materials price increase cause unemployment? If real wages were really flexible, they would come down easily. When the price of one factor of production went up, the economy could adjust by adjusting the price of the other major factor, labor, to the new conditions. But that did not happen in most countries after the first oil shock, because labor markets were geared to rapidly rising wages, both nominal and real. It was a new thing to have an external shock force countries to adjust real wages downwards.

This is a major departure from the Keynesian view of the major cause of unemployment. If unemployment results not just from insufficient demand, but is partly a consequence of the price of labor, institutions have to adjust themselves to this new situation. Some countries are now better adapted. Surprisingly enough, the United States has more flexible real wages than most European countries, because wage contracts in the United States are in nominal terms. These are multi-period contracts, and you don't have formal indexing. When prices rise and existing nominal wages get eaten up by inflation, real wages come down more rapidly. Japan, too, is a country that seems to have adjusted much better than Europe in that respect, but here the reason may simply be that Japan's productivity growth in the past was so much faster that it could live with a much slower rise in real wages. What I would like to emphasize is that the ability of countries to adjust to these new types of shocks has in part, at least, been connected with the ability to be more flexible in wages policy.

When we come to view the prospects for recovery, we have to ask ourselves whether there is a chance that we've solved some of these problems through the traumatic experience of the past ten years. Inflation seems to have been squeezed out of the system for a while, but will inflationary expectations be rekindled once economic activity picks up again? It's hard to say. But I'd like to look at the supply side factors that I mentioned earlier. Oil prices. There is a good chance that we now have sufficient oil reserves and that the excess supply of oil will prevent prices from going up again rapidly in the next two or three years the way they did in 1979–80 during the Iran crisis. But we should remember that we are holding this interview in the Middle East, and in the Middle East you can never predict events. You might suddenly have a political or military crisis causing a disruption of oil supplies. But if we suppose that there is no factor that will endanger oil supplies in the near future, it looks as if oil markets are in a better shape now than they have been for quite some time. No one can guarantee that we will not run into a strengthening of cartels in the oil market in the medium-run, however. Four or five years from now we might have another oil price shock. This might happen, for example, if low oil prices result in lax conservation policies and if the positive developments in the energy field in recent years are halted or reversed. There's no guarantee, in other words, that we will not have another oil price shock in a few years.

Other raw materials have gone up and then come down again. It's not so much a question of whether the rise in oil prices has harmed the world economy as that the fluctuations have done so: responses to a rise in raw materials prices and responses to a fall in raw materials prices are not symmetric. That's part of the problem with responsive macro-economic policy.

Fluctuations in raw materials prices are connected with exchange rate policies and fluctuations in relative exchange rates. And the underlying reasons for the fluctuations in exchange rates have not been eliminated from the system. As long as we have countries operating their own internal monetary policies and not coordinating monetary and exchange rate policies with one another, there's no guarantee that the dollar will not continue to fluctuate against the yen and the mark the way it has done over the past two years. And that in turn has its repercussions on the relative prices on the world market of both raw materials and finished goods.

Talk of the need to return to something that resembles the Bretton Woods system of exchange rates is partly connected with that. You might say that the European Monetary Union is a way of bridging over exchange rate fluctuations within a subset of industrial countries, but as long as you have these sharp fluctuations amongst the major blocs in exchange rates, that problem might come back. And let me again mention the real interest rate issue, which in part, at least, is connected with the exchange rate problem.

At the moment, output and economic activity look like they are picking up and inflation has come down substantially, and my guess would be that there are better prospects for growth in the next few years than there have been in the recent past, but I think the basic institutional problems that we've had are still with us. And the main institutional or political problem is the coordination of macro-economic policies amongst major industrial countries.

On an international scale . . . ,

On an international scale. As long as there's no clear guarantee that countries will coordinate their financial and fiscal policies among them in a more efficient way than they seem to have done in the 1970's and the beginning of the 1980's, we may see a recurrence of some of the problems that we've had before.

To what extent has the world system, or have economies, learned from past mistakes? As I've said, real wages responded downward better after OPEC II than after OPEC I, and this may point to some learning. With OPEC I there was no previous experience to learn from and unemployment was perceived as Keynesian unemployment—so why bring down real wages?—whereas the next time around there was OPEC I to learn from. But perhaps the fact that unemployment was so much higher also helps account for the fact that real wages were more flexible. Again, there are differences among countries—there's been less downward real wage flexibility in most European countries than there has been in the United States or Japan.

We haven't, of course, said anything about unemployment as such. When we talk about prospects for recovery, it's recovery of output and economic activity. When we come to ask what the chances are of unemployment coming down rapidly, I think one has to be more pessimistic. We know that even with a rate of growth of 3 percent or 3½ percent, which is a lot for OECD countries, unemployment would come down only very slowly, if at all. We have a legacy from the 1970's of a very high unemployment rate, and I don't predict much change in the 1980's. That's a major social and political problem. Does it mean that the industrial world has now got to live with an average unemployment rate of 8 or 9 percent as a normal fact of life and that people just have to adjust their ways of life to the fact that part of society is unemployed, or does it mean that more people will be employed, but that they will all be employed for fewer hours? Will there be some social agreement to divide the given number of hours amongst more people? These are social and institutional problems we've inherited from the 1970's, and I don't see a clear way out yet.

You have a certain opinion about the influence of technical change in this respect?

Well, on technical change I think there are two things to be said. I would broaden the question somewhat and talk about productivity, not only technical change. And one of the puzzles of the past decade is the fact that productivity growth in all industrial countries came down sharply after 1973. This is productivity measured in terms both of total GDP per unit of labor and total GDP per unit of labor and capital combined. Whichever way you want to measure it, it seems pretty clear that productivity growth has come down. The question is, why has this happened?

I would argue that this is partly connected with the supply shocks we talked about. When you have a raw material price increase or an oil price increase impinging on the system, that by itself will cause productivity per unit of labor and capital to come down for reasons of technology. But that is only part of the story. Another part is the response, the fact that by and large governments in the industrial countries responded to these shocks by cutting domestic demand. So you had much sharper fluctuations in output in industrial countries after the first oil shock—ever since, in fact—than you had in the 1950's and 1960's. And when output fluctuates more than usual, the productivity in the use of factors comes down and that's part of the reason for the fall in productivity.

Just to substantiate that argument, let's compare the behavior of the industrial countries with the behavior of the industrializing countries during this same period. The latter did not cut back on their economic activity because they borrowed very heavily from the OPEC surplus. And, in fact, productivity in those countries did not come down the way it did in the industrial countries. This goes to show that demand management and productivity are connected. What I said just now has no longer been true for the industrializing countries over the past two or three years. They have been running into trouble with rising real interest rates.

Now, technical change is connected with that story, I think, in at least, well, in more than one way, but let me mention one. It can be argued that when you have a sharp rise in oil prices, in energy prices— and that's also true for other raw materials, but it's particularly true in the energy field—then the oil ways in which you produce output with energy-using equipment are no longer applicable, and there is a strong tendency to go into energy-saving equipment. That's one way in which the productive structure adjusts to the new relative prices in the world system. Changing the structure of equipment is

a way in which countries adjust to external shocks. Now, some of
that has certainly taken place. I mean . . . it's an interesting question
to ask. Has the rate of technical change altered? Is the productivity
slowdown connected with a fall in the rate of growth of technical
progress? I would say no, although I'm sure some people would argue
yes—that part of the productivity slowdown comes from our having
reached a technology frontier and not being able to expand further.
I don't buy that argument. I think that if the world would find a way
of stabilizing its output growth and overcoming the coordination
problem among countries and perhaps stabilize oil markets and raw
materials markets, it would find that productivity growth could in
principle be as fast as it was in "normal" periods. I wouldn't argue
that the end of the sixties was a normal period—there we had an
excessive boom. But say part of the fifties and sixties. So technical
change and productivity growth are not separate issues.

Macro-economic management is where the main problems lie.

In conclusion:

*The conversation with Professor Bruno demonstrates an emphasis on problems
occurring on a world-wide scale relating to the supply side of the economy.
There is an originality in his focus on the shocks which have occurred in the
areas of costs for production factors: great increases in real wages, real interest
rates and real prices of raw materials. Each one of these shocks, and their
combined effect, were more than the system could take. Professor Bruno expects
these shocks to be less, on the one hand, and on the other expects a world
economy which will be better prepared for these exogenous shocks than it was
in the past. He, nevertheless, fears the recurrence of many old problems.*

Professor Lawrence R. Klein was born in Nebraska, in 1920. He is Professor of Economics at the University of Pennsylvania, Philadelphia. In 1980 he received the Nobel prize in Economics, particularly for his contribution to the development of econometric models for the United States and the world economy. Early on in his career he became a follower of Keynesian theory. He received his Doctorate from M.I.T. in Cambridge in 1944. He still directs the economic research being done at the Wharton School of Economics in Philadelphia.

AN INTERVIEW WITH

LAWRENCE R. KLEIN

PENNSYLVANIA

Professor Heertje: *Would you please give us your outlook on the world economy for the coming decade?*

Professor Klein: Well, the group with which I'm associated, the Wharton Econometrics Group, is, I would say, fairly optimistic about the world recovery. The world has been in a crisis—is probably still in a crisis—but it's coming out, and the United States is further along than most of the other major industrial countries in pulling out. The recovery of the United States is quite strong, and every week we get a new batch of confirming estimates. Now, of course, all of that is very short run, that means recovery this year and next year. And if you look around the world you would say there is great pessimism in Europe, quite a bit of optimism in North America, and a lot of optimism in the Pacific, I mean the Pacific Basin, the Pacific Rim countries. Other parts of the world are in kind of a mixed position at the moment. But one thing to keep in mind is that the world very rarely has a whole ten year span or decade of growth without some very significant interruptions. And there is still the concept of the world business cycle or country business cycle. In my own group, for our projections for the United States for the next decade, we have estimated that in 1986 or 1987 there will be a cyclical correction again. That's fairly normal. We may have a hard time pinpointing that at the moment, but there will be some correction. In fact, that's been one of the main points of some of our criticism against the Reagan Administration—that in the beginning they just planned indefinitely, year-after-year, of growth and expansion with no correction. And the correction came so early that it threw all their plans off track. We think that this is a durable recovery, but in terms of the business cycle it would last until about '86 or '87, have a slowing period or adjustment period, and then begin recovering again.

But the other dimension of it is that we aren't projecting a very strong recovery, even though, in the United States at the present time, people say that this particular month of May or June [1983], or this particular quarter, looks very strong. Some people are even characterizing it as a barn burner. In that respect, it looks strong in comparison with what we've had, but in comparison with the kind of typical recovery from a recession, it's very modest. The projections for the decade, for the 1980s, are for about one point slower growth than we've had in the past with several points more on the inflation rate—even though it's come down considerably from its former very high levels—and a relatively high level of unemployment throughout the world. That makes it very different.

Another very important point to keep in mind is that in the past, in an era that we now look upon as very favorable (the fifties and sixties), the developing countries and the socialist countries did better than the world average and the industrial countries were just at the world average, in some periods, or just below. And as we look ahead, the industrial countries set the world average on this lower level, but the developing countries are expected to be slightly below the world average. And that really is the basic problem that the world is facing now—how to accommodate the developing countries and how to deal with their aspirations. They formerly had visions of a development decade of about 6 percent growth; we are now being told that they are not likely to do better than maybe 4 percent, or something like that. It means there will be very little improvement of living standards. And in some areas, particularly the African countries, there is a very dismal outlook. So the problem of accommodating the developing countries, getting them started toward a higher standard of living, is probably going to be our most serious problem. The industrial countries by themselves will recover, and they are doing so, even though the Europeans are terribly pessimistic about this. The socialist countries have all laid plans for a very modest recovery, much lower growth than in the past and much below the capitalist countries.

The reason for this changed relationship among the main countries is that a number of the developing countries got into financial problems, like the Mexican, Argentinian, and Brazilian problems in particular, but more countries have it. And among the communist countries, the Poles got into this problem, not being able to carry a large debt, not being able to make large service payments and expand at the same time. That is causing them to retract in order to reduce their balance of payments deficits and accommodate their loan obligations. It's not certain that they are all going to be successful in making it, but in the process of trying to make it, they tend to introduce policies of restraint. On the part of the developing countries, that is being forced on them by the world banking system. On the part of the socialist countries, it's coming about because they are afraid of disastrous entanglements with financial institutions of the West. And I think, in some respects, the socialist countries decided to go very strongly for high technology and importing sophisticated capital and also raw materials from the West. They are now taking a look at that and saying that it is not such a favorable route. If you recall, when China first normalized relations with the United States in the late seventies, there was an expectation that they would have year-after-year growth of 7 or 8 percent and become a big market for the industrial countries. They've watched the developments in Eastern Europe and decided that they would not want to get into such a difficult situation; so they're now cutting back plans. They have cancelled a lot of projects and they are being very modest in their aspirations. They are settling for growth targets around 4, 5, or 6 percent. And they are on the high side in the socialist world. So we have the socialist world and the developing world being held back by these burdens that they have assumed. The industrial countries have been having a hard time getting rid of the inflation problem, so they have slowed down. It's an entire world slow-down.

If we could come back for a moment to the situation in the Western economies, would you say that the recovery, for example in the United States, is also due to the policy of the Reagan administration or just the opposite?

Well, my interpretation is the opposite. Many people would say that now that the economy is recovering, and recovering strongly, it must mean that the Reagan administration did things right. But I would look at it this way and say if you push a country down so far and generate a big recession by faulty policies, then eventually there will be a recovery. The policies of the Reagan Administration are somewhat better now than they were in 1981 and 1982. That means that we're allowed to have some recovery. For example, many officials of the Reagan Administration did not want to help the developing countries that got into trouble with their debt payments about one year ago. In many public statements and at meetings I went to they said, well, we'll teach them a lesson. They said it was a problem of the developing countries to extricate themselves from their own excesses. Now they realize that it is a world problem. And I think that the one person who realized this was Paul Volcker. He impressed this on the administration and forced them to be more lenient and accommodating, by making a set of negotiations and deals between the International Monetary Fund and the private banks and the main governments involved, including the U.S. government, in such a way that there would be a continuous supply of funds to the countries just to pay the interest on their outstanding loans. This is not necessarily a settled matter. It enabled us to get through 1982, 1983, and probably 1984. But it remains to be seen what the long-run settlement is going to be. But the U.S. recovery, I think, is secure and will go on. It's certainly secure for next year, which is an election year, and we're not likely to have any repressive measures. But you could say that in many respects the Reagan administration got us into a mess, and now we're getting out. In economics we always distinguish between the level of a position and the rate of change. At the present time, our levels are poor but our rate of change is very favorable. The rate of change is favorable because we were depressed so much.

But hasn't it been important to bring down the rate of inflation over the years 1981 and 1982?

I think that's important. The question is whether it was too repressive. That is, you would say, did you have to have such a big recession and so much unemployment in order to do it? And secondly you would have to say that it was handled very clumsily. It was clumsy because the Reagan administration pursued a fiscal policy that was not anti-inflationary, and then, more or less from the sidelines, forced the Federal Reserve into a policy that was anti-inflationary, and it succeeded. But it succeeded by working against this fiscal policy, and that made the correction very severe in terms of unemployment.

Given these facts, is the recovery due to strong monetary policy in the long-run perspective, or not?

Well, yes, but there is a point of view, or an interpretation, of how the economy works, and a point of view of the philosophy. The Reagan administration's philosophy is that it is all embedded in the monetary structure, through monetarism. It is control of the money supply that does it. The other view is more eclectic, and I think more correct, saying that the monetary influences are important, but also the real influences, namely the supply of oil relative to demand, the supply of food relative to demand, and the supply of other basic materials are also important. Just before the Reagan administration came into power, oil prices started heading down and food prices were stabilized. And I think that contributed half the battle.

Secondly, the reason the monetary policies were successful is that it caused so much unemployment. People feared for their job security and were willing to take very moderate wage settlements. Now if you really pin things down to specific acts of the Reagan administration, I would say there are two that were very important. But people don't really recognize these. One act was the decontrol of oil prices in January 1981. That accelerated a movement that the Carter administration had started, and it induced higher oil prices with so much conservation on the part of the public that we cut back from a point of importing about 7 million barrels a day to a low point of between 3 and 4. Now it's between 4 and 5. That cutback was very important in helping our own exchange position in foreign trade and also indicative as to what was going on in the world, and that brought down oil prices.

The second thing the Reagan administration did was to take a very tough stand in the air controllers' strike. That was a signal to the trade union movement that there was going to be a very tough attitude toward labor, kind of a no-nonsense attitude. I think that broke the back of trade union resistance to a large extent. It turns out to have been a fairly successful gambit against labor, and it's had a lot of effect on wage restraint. Now in many respects, Mrs. Thatcher did the same thing in the United Kingdom, took a very tough stand on public service employees and other trade union negotiations and brought down the growth of wage rates to levels that were consistent with a lower rate of inflation. Now I personally would attribute much more significance to those things than to tight money, by itself, as ways to bring down inflation. Now the part of the world that came through these adjustment periods best were the Asian countries. After the Iranian revolution and the second rise in oil prices, Japanese workers, through various kinds of negotiations, agreed to wage increases in the order of magnitude of 5 to 6 percent. With those low wages, the Japanese were able to bring inflation under control pretty quickly. And that's in contrast to the way things worked out in 1974 and 1975 for Japan. The other Asian nations also held wages in check, and that held down prices. I think, in fact, that the Japanese workers held back on money wages and came out ahead on real wages, taking into account purchasing power. This has probably been the most significant thing. So the wage-labor market policies have, in my opinion, been the key to the situation.

So if we look into the future, the question may arise: what can we expect with respect to labor and wage claims in general, and in particular in Japan? Could we expect that in Japan the situation will be more or less like that we have experienced in Europe and perhaps partly in the United States.

I don't know, but you'd have to argue that if Japanese workers adopted the procedures of European and American workers, adopted our ideals and standards, if we were to Americanize the Japanese trade union movement, we would indeed gain some competitive advantage. I really don't know what's going to happen. I think the reason that the adjustment is so difficult in Europe at the present time is that European workers are much more traditional and working much more by the rules—traditional rules—than American and Japanese workers, and the adjustment is harder. I think that's what gives rise to the pessimism in Europe. Europeans are very pessimistic. They feel there's been a structural change and that the economies are locked into a crisis, that no kind of recovery will be durable. I spent all last week in Paris in meetings citing the kind of numbers we're having in the United States. First they found them unbelievable, but then if you documented that these were the American figures, they'd take the attitude that it couldn't happen in Europe, because there have

been too many structural and institutional changes, making it difficult to get people to accept moderate wages and accept an adjustment
that would allow Europe to go ahead very fast. I think Europeans
have overdone pessimism. The American outlook of reasonable
recovery that is durable and that goes on is probably pretty good—
with business cycle adjustments. Every decade that we've been through
since the end of World War II has seen some unexpected blow-up—
the Korean War and the Vietnam War and the oil embargo and things
like that. So you don't know what's in store for the rest of the decade
of the eighties, but something like prior disturbances could happen.
Barring something like that, and just accepting a normal cyclical
correction, I would say that we look for moderate growth in the
United States. That's considered very optimistic in Europe at the
present time. I want to say one more thing: the view of a moderate
recovery is the consensus at the moment; most people are taking this
attitude. But there is a possibility that everything may work out
much stronger; that everybody is being too pessimistic. The strength
comes from the new technical developments. Those things are the
microelectronics revolution, the bio-engineering possibilities, health
delivery systems, the green revolution and further developments in
agriculture, the whole information system that has spun off the
microelectronics revolution, and some other things we haven't thought
of. Those that I cited are the ones that people talk about. If you take
the attitude that all the developments in those sectors have not been
exploited, and are just beginning to be exploited, then you would
say that there's a pretty good future ahead, but people just aren't able
to see it yet. But the way microelectronics is taking over now in the
United States on such a huge scale, the way the information industry
is blossoming, I would say there are seeds for very significant expansion, and probably in two or three years these might begin to take
hold.

*That would also be my personal view, I must say. Don't you think that the
present strong recovery here in the United States—stronger than anybody
thought, a few months ago, say—is also on the whole due to technology?*

No, I think that what we're seeing now in the United States is a
cyclical recovery. Once the interest rates began to come down, the
Federal Reserve and Paul Volcker really did turn around. They turned

around last July [1982] when the administration agreed to some tax increases. Then they turned around again after the Mexican problem, and they started pumping more reserves into the banking system because too many American banks were exposed in that situation. Interest rates fell considerably. We've been having a big turn around in housing, and we have consumer spending increasing; then we have the Reagan defense program. Inventory investment has been a little bit slow, but it is now starting to rebuild. Among the things that go with housing—consumer durable spending—we see increases. I don't think that's so much due to the new technologies as to the normal cyclical recovery.

But it is a fact that there is a stronger recovery than one could have predicted a few months ago.

In the range of predictions, the Wharton predictions from my own group were always in the upper quartile in distribution range, so we don't feel surprised. We've been fighting with the officials, the government economists, on this issue. I wrote some articles for the media saying that they took a low forecast in order to put some restrictions on spending for social services and things like that. They deny this. But I think they purposely took too conservative a stance. Everything was there, everything was evident that the recovery would be fairly good, as it is now. This is not a wild recovery, it's just quite solid, and it seems to be firmly in place. The next step is to get more private investment, and that seems to be happening at the moment. Personally, and I think from the point of view of careful study, that what we're getting now in the United States isn't surprising. If the new technologies were to have their full impact, then we would get small boom conditions. But that will be a complicated thing, because in the beginning we would have the boom to make, let us say, robots, to make sophisticated electronic hardware. But once it's in place and you've used up a lot of worker hours in the manufacturing, then we have to face up to the problem of how to deal with advanced productivity techniques that require fewer workers.

That's the normal consequence of technology, isn't it?

Yes, it is. Now my feeling is that when that happens, we should work toward a shorter working week. But not before about 1985 or

1986. We might cut about three to five hours off the work week, taking the gains for more leisure. That's not the only solution, but that would be one solution.

A shorter work week based on the productivity of the new technology, not as they discuss it in Europe, as you know—just to have a shorter work week without looking at technology.

The shorter work week now discussed in Europe is to share the unemployment and I'm not very sympathetic with that. To share the productivity gains is the real thing. But that doesn't come for about two or three years.

Thank you very much.

In conclusion:

Professor Klein's answers to the general questions are cogent and lucid; they also contain a broad world vision which is striking. He is fairly optimistic because, in his opinion, recovery is more or less in the nature of things. Important here is his statement that it is not so much Mr. Reagan's penny pinching, but his hard line policy against the unions which has been crucial. Aside from this, Klein clearly demonstrates a multifaceted view of the economic situation. He, also, is a typical econometrician, illustrating his words with figures at all times.

Professor Milton Friedman was born in New York, in 1912. He is presently Research Professor with the Hoover Institute at Stanford University. Before that he had been a professor at the University of Chicago since 1948. In 1976 he received the Nobel prize in Economics, particularly for his work in the area of economic theory.

Professor Friedman can be regarded as the founder of monetarism, the concept that disturbances in the economy have their cause in monetary issues. In this context in particular, an over-expansion of the money supply, which also finances a nominal increase in transactions, is central. According to Friedman, the Central Bank ought to determine the growth of money supplies by percentage, so that only real growth of the economy is financed. He is of the opinion that this growth in the money supply is sufficient to steer the economy in the right direction.

Professor Friedman has received numerous Honorary Doctorates. They also demonstrate his contributions to economics in areas other than monetary theory.

AN INTERVIEW WITH

MILTON FRIEDMAN

STANFORD

Professor Heertje: *I would be most interested in your views on the current relations between the U.S.A. and the world economy.*

Professor Friedman: The world economy consists of a collection of individual countries. There are influences that affect them all, but there are also very important influences that affect individual countries. I believe, therefore, that it is oversimplistic to talk about world recovery, world economic conditions, world recession. We have to consider particular countries. So far as the United States is concerned, we are currently in a very strong recovery.

Unfortunately, I have no great confidence that that recovery will be long lasting. I believe the monetary explosion we have had over the past year is likely to mean either an acceleration of inflation in 1984–85, or else that the monetary authorities will shortly step very hard on the brakes and that we shall have renewed recession sometime in mid-1984. What happens over the longer period for the United States depends critically on which of these two alternatives occur and precisely when they occur.

There is nothing wrong with the basic economy of the United States that a period of relatively stable monetary policy, a period without strong inflationary pressure, would not cure. So there are very good underlying prospects on the real level for the next ten years or so. The only question is whether they will be realized, given the unsatisfactory character of the monetary and fiscal policies we have been pursuing.

With respect to other countries, I believe the prospects for Great Britain are among the most favorable. Britain has followed a very tough policy of squeezing inflation out of the economy. It has paid a very high cost for doing so. But it is now on the verge, I believe, of being able to realize those costs.

The situation in Japan is one of the most complex. Japan has been a relatively healthy economy. It has done an extraordinary good job of monetary management since 1973. As a result it has relatively little inflation pressure and responded very well to the second oil shock. The problem is that Japan has been imitating the other Western countries in one very dangerous respect. Government spending has been rising rapidly in Japan. A decade or two ago, when Japan was growing at 10 percent a year in real terms, government spending in Japan was less than half of American spending as a fraction of income. It is now approaching American spending and may soon exceed it. As a result, real growth in Japan has been slowing down very rapidly. There are strong pressures within Japan to resist these tendencies and it is an open question whether they will succeed in doing so. As a result, I am nothing like so optimistic about the future of Japan as are many of the people who comment on it.

So far as continental Europe is concerned, you have France on the one side in which the socialist government has been forced to do a U-turn and shift from policies of Keynesian expansionism to policies of Thatcherite restraint. Will Mitterand and his government be able to carry that policy through? Germany has been seriously hampered by its participation in the European monetary system, which has forced it, essentially, to provide subsidies to some fellow members within that association by supporting their currencies. For political reasons, Germany feels that it must retain that European monetary system. As a result, the outlook for Germany is fairly clouded.

In short, I find I have the greatest confidence in judging what happens in the United States, where I know the most, and the least confidence in judging what is going to happen on the continent of Europe, about which I know the least.

On the basis of what you have said, I would very much like to have your opinion about the development of the international currency system. What will happen—will we stick to a combination of flexible and fixed currencies? And what would be your global view on, for example, the development of the dollar to the English pound and the yen. Because I think on the basis of what you have said that you must have some indication in mind.

Despite all the talk about international monetary conferences and a new Bretton Woods, I believe there will be no basic change in the international monetary system over the coming decade at least. The floating exchange rate system, "dirty floating," in which various countries intervene is not the pure floating that persons like myself would desire, but it is a floating rate system nonetheless, and it has been working extremely well.

It enabled the world to cope effectively with the financial consequences of the Arab oil crisis. Moreover, while many people express dissatisfaction with the present system, while there are many suggestions for change, and while you might even get a majority who believe it desirable to have change, there is no consensus on what form the change should take. Various groups want very different changes. Therefore, this system will continue to survive very much in its present form.

As to the relative importance of different currencies, that depends on what happens internally in the various countries. If the United States were to continue the erratic monetary policy that has characterized the past several decades, with a roller coaster of inflation, around an upward trend, the dollar would continue to lose its status as the key currency in the system. On the other hand, if the United States can maintain a policy over the next few years in which inflation, while it may temporarily rise a little, as it undoubtedly will in 1984 and 1985, comes back down and stays down in single digits, then I suspect the U.S. dollar will continue to be the primary currency used around the world for many transactions and for intervention purposes. As to the other currencies involved, the German mark has lost much of its appeal. If I am right about what I believe will happen in Britain, then I believe the British pound will regain a more important role as an important international currency. London remains a major international financial center; it will remain that and probably become more important.

It may also be that the yen will assume a greater role as an international currency, given the fact that the Japanese have been making considerable progress in freeing their money in capital markets from the kinds of restrictions that have kept the yen a fairly isolated currency.

It's worth noting that in the sixties and seventies there was a world-wide inflationary trend. The world learned the lesson that an inflationary process is not a very satisfactory one; that far from contributing to full employment, it leads to higher unemployment over the longer period. So in the early 1980s, there has been, throughout the world, a shift in priorities and the adoption of policies directed at reducing inflation. That has, so far, had considerable success almost everywhere. Inflation has either stopped going up or has started to come down and has come down fairly drastically in Britain, in the United States, and in some other countries. A great deal depends on whether, in countries around the world as well as the United States, that shift in priorities is successful in producing a relatively noninflationary monetary policy or turns out to be a temporary change—a real possibility in view of the transitional costs, in the form of unemployment and lower output, associated with bringing down inflation.

Do you think that, say since the beginning of the eighties, the influence of so-called monetarist policies and monetarism on policy making has increased, and are you happy with the results or not?

It's extremely important to distinguish between words and acts, between rhetoric and deeds. Every central bank around the world in the past four or five years has adopted monetarist rhetoric. Almost none of them have adopted a monetarist policy. The only central bank that has adopted an effective monetarist policy, in my opinion, has been the Bank of Japan. And interestingly enough, while their policy has come closer to monetarist views, their rhetoric has been less so. A key element of monetarist policy is not only giving primary attention to the quantity of money, but, much more important, achieving steadiness and predictability in the growth of the quantity of money. A fundamental monetarist principle is that a stable monetary structure requires a commitment to a stated and predictable rate of monetary growth. When you are in an inflationary period, as we were in the seventies, the monetarist position is that the rate of monetary growth should be slowed, but in a steady, gradual, and predictable way. The Japanese have done that. The United States, which proclaimed itself attached to monetarist rhetoric, has not. On the contrary, monetary growth in the United States during the past three years has been more unstable than during any other three-year period in the Federal Reserve's history. In Britain as well, although the rhetoric was monetarist, the actual policy was not. Monetary growth was anything but steady, it was very unstable. The *average* rate of growth was reduced in both Britain and the United States and that is why inflation came down. But the instability in monetary growth meant that the costs of reducing inflation were very much greater than they need have been. If the same reduction in average growth had been produced steadily, economic conditions would have been stabler, interest rates would have been lower, and unemployment rates would have been lower than they were. As to whether monetarism has gained or lost, there has been no effect on monetarist theory or the evidence for monetarist propositions; if anything, the experience of the past few years has simply provided another bit of confirmatory evidence on the importance of the quantity of money. However, the public reputation of monetarism has unquestionably declined as a result of the difference between monetarist rhetoric and actual policy. In a paper I wrote some time ago, I said that if the Federal Reserve system of the United States had set out with the deliberate purpose of discrediting monetarism, it would not have behaved any differently than it did. It's worth emphasizing that although the Federal Reserve system in the United States used monetarist rhetoric, not a single member of the Federal Reserve board is, or ever has been, a monetarist.

In conclusion:

While many think that Friedman's ideas are firmly rooted and, thus, determine policy in the United States and England, Friedman himself is of the opinion that his ideas receive only lip-service. He seems, in general, nevertheless, rather optimistic about the current state of affairs. Notable is his opinion on Japan, which, on the one hand, express the idea that Japan has, indeed, followed a monetarist policy, and on the other, the idea that the growth of government spending is causing too great a pressure there.

Professor John Kenneth Galbraith was born in Ontario, Canada, in 1908. He was a professor at Harvard University from 1946 to 1975. In 1934 he received his Doctorate from the University of California at Berkeley.

Professor Galbraith's fame stems somewhat less from his contributions to economic theory than his often unorthodox way of treating explosive social issues, for which he has a special talent. He became quite well known with the publication in 1958 of his book *The Affluent Society*. In it he states that the relative luxury we derive from goods in the private sector stands in contradistinction to poverty in the public sector, as the government is incapable of providing for the collective public needs. Aside from this theme, his book devoted considerable attention to environmental issues before it was considered fashionable. Many of Galbraith's writings have influenced political platforms, especially those of a liberal orientation.

A publication of the Wiardi-Beckman Foundation in the Netherlands, titled *Om de kwaliteit van het bestaan* (The quality of life), written by Drs. J.M. den Uyl (Prime Minister of the Netherlands from 1973–1977), was inspired by Galbraith.

JOHN KENNETH GALBRAITH

HARVARD

Professor Heertje: *Professor Galbraith, the purpose of the interview is to get your view of the present economic situation and, more particularly, your opinion as to whether the economic recovery, if there is one, will last, and what kind of economic problems we may face in the future. We are not thinking in terms of the coming months but more of the coming years. I would very much like to have your reaction to that.*

Professor Galbraith: Well, you know what Keynes said: in the long run, we're all dead . . . . So I can speak on that with great confidence in the knowledge that very few people will be around to correct me—if it's a long enough run. I'm always a bit reluctant about forecasting because one must bear in mind that people make forecasts, economists make forecasts, not because they know but because they're asked. And if all the economic forecasts were right, all uncertainty would leave the system and free enterprise, capitalism, would come to an end, wouldn't it?

Yes, that's true, I think.

So, as you see I never make forecasts without a suitable prefatory apology. But I should not be in doubt as to what is happening now. The administration of Mr. Reagan came to power just under three

years ago with two deeply conflicting ideas. There were on the one
hand the supply-side economists, as they were called, who held that
the problem of the modern economy was one of incentives. Putting
it in rather blunt terms, they held that in the United States the poor
were not working because they had too much money and the rich
were not working because they had too little money. And so they
proposed to reinvigorate the economy by cutting the taxes on the
rich and cutting the benefits for the poor. That was one group that
came to Washington. The other group, under the influence of my
friend Professor Milton Friedman, held that the modern economy
in all its complexity could be regulated by having a tight hold on the
money supply, relating that to growth and the gross national product,
and that this would combine stable prices, perhaps not with full
employment, but with an acceptable level of unemployment, whatever that may be. Well, the change that has occurred in the last three
years comes about as the result of the rejection of both of these
groups. First, supply-side economics has given way to a renewed
understanding of the extent to which capitalism depends on a com-
passionate attitude to the people it ignores and neglects. We're having
a return to a concern for economic welfare. And it was discovered
that while monetary policy in a highly organized economy works
against inflation, it only works if you have a great deal of unemployment as a restraining force on the trade unions, if you have a great
deal of idle plant capacity as a restraining force on the capacity of
modern oligopolies to raise prices, if you have a lot of small business
failure, if, indeed, you have a great deal of hardship.

So we've had a reversal of the monetary policy, a very substantial
reversal. Professor Friedman has said, "If the policy now be monetarism, I am no longer a monetarist."

And the supply-side economists have given way to a new and
extravagant Keynesianism, with very large public deficits inspired
not by welfare expenditure, to be sure, but by military expenditure.
When you reverse the wrong policies, when you reverse the policy
of monetary restraint and when you go over to a policy of saying
that public deficits are acceptable as Keynes did, you get a changed
prospect. And indeed we have one now, and one consequence is that
we're having quite a respectable rate of recovery. It is not, however,
a rate of recovery that is doing a great deal to solve the problem of

unemployment. Because it's quite clear we have structural conditions in some of our older industries that, as Professor Leontief has said, to some extent resemble the problem of the horse after the tractor became common in agriculture. Horses became unemployed and no change in the agricultural situation would bring those horses back into work. In our older industries, we have, in addition to the macro-economic problem, structural problems of unemployment, which I would not expect to see solved by this administration. But as long as we have a strongly Keynesian fiscal policy, a retreat from mone-tarism, and no internal collapse, I would rather expect the recovery to continue.

You don't, then, see the problem of inflation coming up again?

That's the question I was expecting you to ask.

I would not be in any doubt on that point if the recovery continues, under the pressure of the military spending, and permitted by low interest rates (real interest rates are still high by past standards but low as compared with what they have been), we will certainly have a resumption of inflation. We'll have two forms of inflation in the modern economy. We'll have a return to the inflation that comes from the pressure of demand on prices, and we'll have what is more im-portant, a return to the inflation which is the result of the income/prices spiral. Were I to venture a forecast, it would be that in the months ahead we will have a substantial jump in prices in the United States . . .

Even in the months ahead already?

In the months ahead. And that the Reagan administration will be caught in an election year with the problem of whether to go to the country with a tight money policy to control inflation or whether to accept the inflation and the higher level of output and employment that might go with it. Some of my economic friends have been cap-tured by what I have come to call the "peristalsis theory of inflation." The peristalsis theory of inflation deals with inflation by analogy to bodily processes. It holds that once you have given the economic system a very large dose of medicine such as castor oil, you extrude the inflationary danger and it's gone forever. I don't believe that. I'm persuaded that as the recovery continues we will have the underlying force of demand-push or demand-pull and wage/price-push inflation back again.

Don't you think that the present policies of the Federal Reserve are meant to avoid that situation?

Certainly not. Nobody should imagine that the Federal Reserve is blessed by God with a special dispensation to combine full employment with stable prices.

No, but don't you think they are trying to right that situation?

No question that they are trying. But you have to believe in magic, in black magic, before you can suppose that Mr. Volcker and his fellow board members and the open market committee are capable of necromancy.

Is it perhaps possible that in this case the black magic will turn out to be a technical change?

This is something I should never have to argue with a Dutchman. You are known to be down-to-earth, practical people who long ago rejected the role of the spiritual power in human affairs. Only someone who believes deeply in the power of prayer could imagine that the Federal Reserve acting alone is capable of combining full employment with stable prices.

No, but I come back to my point. Wouldn't it be possible that technical change may lead to a subsequent increase in productivity on the one hand and many more new products on the other, so that the problem of inflation will be, well, at least less bad and less serious than without technical change?

I don't believe it for a moment, but I must urge you not to go to Washington because there you'll find any number of people wanting to escape from reality and anxious to believe it.

But still, I would think that there being so much new technology and so many new technical insights available that they could be applied in such a way that there would be unforeseen rises in the level of productivity.

Nothing can be ruled out in this world, but one cannot readily imagine the prospect of such a technical change. We used to say in the United States that when the liberal imagination failed in all other matters, it advocated enforcement of the anti-trust laws. Now we can say that when the conservative imagination fails in all other matters, it says there will be great technical changes that will rescue us.

Well, I am not defending a conservative position, I'm just asking.

You will have no doubt as to my answer.

No, well, I'm a little bit surprised about the answer, I must say. I thought you would emphasize the importance of technical change a little bit more . . .

I don't minimize the importance of technical change, but I don't expect it to work wonders. It hasn't in the past and it won't in the future. And one should bear another thing in mind: the cutting edge of economic change in our time is not technology but design. The great expanding industries in our time are those that depend on good design, on artistic taste. The entertainment industry, the record industry, the music industry, the dress industry: these are the industries where the older countries have had their great expansion. People who talk about the wonders of technology are people who are so blinded that they haven't seen the expansion in the artistic industries. These increasingly capture a greater share of the gross national product. No artist wants to be in the gross national product but, alas, he is. And increasingly in our time.

That's true, but even those industries rely heavily on new technical methods.

You're infatuated with technology, and obviously I can't do anything about it.

No, no . . . Would you . . . What would be your perspective in the coming two years as to unemployment? Do you still think that it will get very high? It's going down a little.

My view on that is essentially orthodox. I think we have had a secular increase in the basic level of unemployment—a secular increase in the number of people who have been rendered obsolete by the transfer of industries—textiles, steel, shipbuilding—to Japan, Korea, Singapore. This is a problem that will continue to afflict us, and its manifestation will be a continuing high level of unemployment in the older industrial areas.

So, you consider the recent developments in unemployment figures in the United States to be temporarily favourable?

Oh, they're certainly not getting worse, but if you examine those figures you'll see that unemployment, in spite of the recovery that has occurred, has declined very little. I was noticing today that some of the figures for the old industrial states such as Michigan and Ohio are still increasing.

I would like to come back for a moment to the real rate of interest. You said in passing that it's high but we can live with it. Is it true that it is in fact really very high compared with the past?

Oh, no question.

And that it also hampers recovery?

There's no question that it continues to be high in relation to the past, and I think one can hold out the possibility that if it continues at the present level it will hamper recovery. On the other hand, if we have a recurrence of inflation, as I would predict, that will have some effect in reducing the real rate. It will mean that people as a practical matter can buy houses or build houses in the knowledge that some part of their borrowing costs will be taken care of by the increase in capital value. And this will be true also of business investment. So you can have a decline in the real rate of interest, either by a decline in the nominal rate or by an increase in inflation.

And I understand that you predict an increase in inflation, hence no decrease in the nominal rates of interest?

I would predict an increase in inflation. Then if the nominal rate stays the same, it would have the effect of reducing the real rate, wouldn't it?

Yes, of course. So in your view then the dollar will remain strong insofar as that depends on the rate of interest?

No, I hesitate to make predictions on that. If the Federal Reserve is persuaded by the administration to hold the rate of interest at something like present levels and we have a recurrence of inflation, then the dollar will not be strong. But you're getting me into an area of prediction where, as I've said, I proceed with a good deal of caution.

I can understand that, but it's just an introduction to discussion of the whole exchange system and, well, the international relationships of currencies and exchange rates and whether we will stick to the present situation or not. Do you think there will again be a change in the whole system? Will gold play a role again? Or will we have another Bretton Woods?

These are political questions that are very hard to answer. I would be quite confident that gold will not again play an important role. Gold has become the intellectual plaything of the people who yearn for the eighteenth century or the nineteenth century, to the extent that they have escaped from Greek and Roman times. The people who say with magnificent solemnity that we must create a new world monetary system, are people who, without exception, I think, do not know what a complex set of policies they are talking about. So I think we can dismiss the role of gold and silver. And the notion of a new Bretton Woods has to contend with the fact that international currency stability is only possible if one has a coordination of internal policies. As long as internal policies are different, wage/price policies

are different, fiscal policies are different, and rates of inflation are
different, we're going to have uneven movements in the exchange
rates. Indeed, we must. Otherwise, the countries with lower rates
of inflation would quickly become devoid of all products as they each
become a bargain place to buy. The one thing that's worse than fixed
exchange rates, the one thing that's worse than unstable exchange
rates is stable exchange rates when you have differing rates of internal
inflation. So, when and if we have a new Bretton Woods, it will have
to be one that also discusses the coordination of internal wage and
price policies and the coordination of internal fiscal and monetary
policies.

*I understand. I have one closing question, if I may. Do I understand that
you foresee the problems you described years ago in* The Affluent Society
coming up again? Do you think, in the first place, that they're still there?

You will have to be more specific.

*Well, for example, the problem of the relationship between the public and the
private sector and the fact that while in the private sector things are now
perhaps getting a little bit better again; in the public sector we are running
out of means to provide people with things relevant to their welfare.*

I published *The Affluent Society* in 1958, twenty-five years ago. I wouldn't
like to insist that everything I said then is still true; Winston Chur-
chill once said, I've often had to eat my words and on the whole I
found them a wholesome diet. I would still adhere very strongly to
two of the major points in *The Affluent Society*. One is that the modern
process of want creation is something that does not grow out of the
inherent character of men and women, but is the highly conditioned
consequence of modern advertising. Along with the production of
goods goes the creation of the demand for the goods. This is something that my fellow economists recognize but have had difficulty
reconciling with their textbooks, and when you have difficulty reconciling something with your textbook, you often ignore it. Given the
massive character of modern want creation, television advertising,
newspaper advertising, merchandising of products, this point is rather
more relevant today than it was when I wrote *The Affluent Society*.

A second thing I would still continue to emphasize is the importance of the environment. One always exaggerates one's own influence, but I think it's fair to say that *The Affluent Society* was one of the first books to argue that we must not only consider increase in the gross national product as a goal, but must protect our surroundings—our air, our water, our countryside—from the adverse effect of economic growth—that the standard of living involves not only goods but our surroundings. The environmental movement is an affirmation of the point I made in *The Affluent Society*. It goes considerably beyond anything I expected. Here in New England there's great concern now about acid rain, sulphur compounds in the rainwater. That was something I did not know about or foresee when I wrote twenty-five years ago.

Thirdly—I said there were two things but let me add another—I urged that we must have a balance between our public consumption and our private consumption, between the public sector and the private sector. I believe that still to be true. I did not, however, see how difficult it was to maintain that balance. Nor did I think it likely then that the balance would get worse. In modern New York, Chicago, Los Angeles, Philadelphia, the balance between public consumption and private consumption is much worse than it was twenty-five years ago when I published that book. New York has a very high level of upper income consumption. Its public services are in appalling condition in many places. The problem of maintaining what I called the social balance was something that I did not foresee—it is far greater than I thought it would be twenty-five years ago.

I see. Do you think that in the coming years this will really still be a very serious problem, because the public sector is now a bit restricted?

I think it will continue to be a serious problem. There has been some change in attitude in the last two or three years. In some ways we have been educated by the present administration in the United States. It came into power with a great commitment to the private sector, against the public sector. In a great many matters, we have learned that this is not consistent with social tranquility and the good life. So there has been some return to an emphasis on the public sector. A few minutes ago I was reading a speech by one of the Democratic candidates on the importance of much greater emphasis on what he calls the public infrastructure, not a term I like to use. He was speaking about this with something approaching passion.

Thank you very much.

In conclusion:

The surprise of this conversation with Galbraith is in his opinion that the arch-conservative Reagan actually follows a Keynesian policy, because of the budget deficit, as well as a flexible monetary policy. Because of this, Galbraith is rather optimistic about the current situation. He is afraid though, that the rate of inflation will rise again, but seems to attach minor importance to it.

As far as the issues he typically raises, such as the tension between private and public sectors, he notes that these are still relevant. The solution, according to him, is to be found in an expansion of the public sector. In this conversation Galbraith, again, comes across as a good journalistic subject.

Professor Robert L. Heilbroner is a Professor in the Department of Economics at the New School of Social Research. He was born in New York, in 1919. He gained notoriety in the Netherlands with his book *The Worldly Philosophers*. In it he humorously discusses the ideas of history's most important economists. Aside from this, he focused mainly on economic analysis of economic theses, such as socialism and communism. Heilbroner is known in the United States as a liberal economist, who from time to time holds a mirror up to American society.

AN INTERVIEW WITH

ROBERT A. HEILBRONER

NEW SCHOOL

Professor Heertje: *Well, as you know, Professor Heilbroner, the question in general is about your views and opinions on the perspective of the world economy; whether you think that the recovery will be sustained or not and what kind of problems you see before us in the future. And I would very much like to have your reaction to that general problem.*

Professor Heilbroner: Well, let me begin by trying to identify four problems that seem to be at the center of this larger question.

The first problem is whether or not the general Keynesian techniques of accelerating economic growth are still effective. Those techniques were certainly useful in the general setting of the late 1930's–early 1940's; but they've unquestionably become less and less effective in the new socioeconomic setting in which inflation rather than massive unemployment is the latent danger. So the question is whether or not we can use expansive techniques without bringing ourselves into an impossible situation of inflation. Expansionary economic policies are today, and will be in the future, essential for a healthy society. I personally believe that, and that they can be combined with the necessary controls to minimize their inflationary consequences. But it must be said that so far no really workable combination has been found.

The second question, it seems to me, is quite separate. It is whether or not modern technology has moved Western countries in general toward a position in which resumption of economic growth is likely to push the labor force out of the industrial and private sector into some kind of limbo—that is into unemployment without any easy exit. The reason I raise the question is because modern-day technology—micro-circuitry and all the rest—brings to the fore the possibility that technological unemployment may become a massive and persistent problem for Western capitalist nations for a very long time, regardless of whether they are successful in resuming growth or not. In fact, one might even say that if they do resume growth, and if there is an investment boom, it may make technological unemployment worse because growth is apt to be based on this technology.

The third problem is again different. It is whether, or how, the international economy is going to find some reasonable degree of stability. In part, this has to do with discovering techniques for reestablishing exchange rates and exchange relationships of a kind that enable international trade and production to take place. It's very clear that the developments of the past ten years have been very destabilizing. There must be some effort to reestablish a kind of Bretton Woods, or whatever it may be. Another aspect of the same question of international living together is whether or not large-scale intercontinental and international competition of the kind we have seen in the past ten years will not also require some new degree of protectionist intervention. It's clear that like the international world of finance, the international world of trade and production is unstable. There have been massive relocations of production: I suppose the most familiar example is the extraordinary rise of Japan, but it's not the only one. And the question is, what are we to do to establish some reasonable degree of domestic market security for industrial nations?

And, finally, the last question I simply raise without any answer: what to do with the continuing problem of the relations between the rich nations and the poor nations?

Those are the questions it seems to me that have to be addressed in order to try to make intelligent comments about what the prospects are for international well-being over the next decade.

May I pick out one of the questions you raised—the problem of technology? Isn't it true that so far we haven't had massive unemployment due to technology and that problems with respect to the labor market have other sources?

Yes, this may be. You know, I think it was Paul Samuelson who once said that the paranoia of the right is government deficits and the paranoia of the left is technological unemployment. And it is true that some reasonable degree of employment opportunities has come side by side with extraordinary technological changes. Just the same, I want to put the other side of the argument. It seems to me, looking back over a hundred years of economic change, that we can see the progressive entrance of technology into three sectors, the agricultural sector, the manufacturing sector, and the private service sector. Technology first enters the agricultural sector with reapers, threshers, harvesters, and improved means of cultivation, and a very large surplus labor force is created on the farms. Everyone knows that a hundred years ago, 50 to 60 percent of the population was in farming. Today it's 3 percent. My question is, where did the people who were displaced from the farms go? And the answer is, by and large they went into "the factory" and into "the office."

Now in the factory, which is the place where technological change next enters, there was a standoff. There was a continuous stream of people from the countryside who quite literally went into the factories, or whose sons left the farm to go to the factory. And there was also a stream of inventions into those factories, conveyors and overhead belts and large-scale machinery, and so forth. The result was a kind of equilibrium of employment. The volume of production increased by leaps and bounds, but the entrance of technology kept the percentage of the work force in the factory approximately level, at least in the United States. In 1900—I'm just taking a rough figure—about a third of the work force was in manufacturing. Today it's a little less than a third.

Now what happened to the "excess" population that went off the farms? The answer is, they went into office work. Whereas in 1900 a quarter of the work force worked in services of all kinds (not just offices of course), by 1982 that number was about 70 percent.

So that was the way we have managed to absorb the impact of

technology in the past. Now comes the problem. The new technology is beginning to enter the service sector. Essentially the new technology is a technology of information and control, a technology of tasks that were formerly white-collar tasks of recognition, filing, and so forth. What is going to happen as technology on the grand scale enters the office, store, or government agency in the way that technology entered the farm and then the factory? If there is an increase in the private demand for new kinds of automatized services or much cheaper services, then fine, there may be enough increase in private employment to keep the situation manageable. But if, as I feel may be the case, the new technology comes in and the secretary and the clerk and the bureaucrat go out, *and there isn't any correspondingly large increase in demand,* into what sector are these displaced persons going to go? The only answer I can think of is some kind of deliberately contrived public service sector: the provision of non-profitable useful tasks, of which there is a great need, whose economic purpose will be to provide employment to people who have no likely chances of finding employment in the private sector. I think that's the present state of affairs. I agree with you that there's no reason to assume that the outcome will be necessarily bad, but it does strike me as being sufficiently new in its configuration, so that it poses a real risk.

I think so, too, in principle, but at least partly it may also lead to a reduction in labor time.

Yes, you're quite right. Another way of coping with it is to change the dimensions of work life. You begin later, you leave sooner, you work less. You know, that's not so easy to do. In the beginning people worked so hard, so many hours, that work was all disutility and exhaustion. When you work as people do now, forty hours a week, in a reasonable job, the work becomes much more than just a disutility; it's the manner in which you define your life. To cut that work way down is to risk taking out of society one of the order-bestowing forces within it. It raises deep questions as to the psychological and social and political stability of a population that doesn't begin to work until say it's twenty-five instead of eighteen and that stops work when it's fifty-five instead of sixty-five, and only works twenty hours a week instead of forty hours a week. The absence of a work focus within daily life may be a source of grave anomie. The long-term goal for society is to enrich and enhance work, not to "abolish" it. So it strikes me that the problem of coping with a thorough change in work life is not so easy. Not impossible; one can have longer vacations, one can have sabbaticals, one can have more participation in decision making. But the shrinkage of work is not an unalloyed blessing.

May we come back to one of the other issues you raised about the exchange rate and the possibility of a new Bretton Woods. Perhaps you could elaborate a little bit on this. I wonder whether you are also thinking of a new role for gold in this respect or just the other way around?

Well, I speak now as an American. Perhaps I exaggerate, but by and large until a very few years ago most Americans did not pay much attention to international finance. This is because they "knew"—and they knew correctly—that when all was said and done, the American dollar was the Rock of Gibraltar. And so foreign finance didn't make any difference, so to speak. It was only a matter for economists, not a matter for ordinary people. Now, as everyone knows, the American dollar is not the Rock of Gibraltar and the question of finding some sort of exchange stability becomes a matter of very great importance for this economy, as it always has been for European economies. When the dollar was still the Rock of Gibraltar, there was a great deal of support for the idea that a freely fluctuating exchange market would work just like a free market where all prices arrive at their own equilibrium levels, which would be in the end for everyone's benefit. When there is no Rock of Gibraltar currency, that idea is no longer so appealing, for freely fluctuating or rapidly fluctuating markets bring short-run speculative opportunities that in turn bring about capital flows that are very disequilibrating, pushing money into, or draining money out of, countries. It's quite clear that it is extremely difficult, maybe impossible, to run a coherent national economic policy when you are exposed to the threat of inflows or outflows of exchange on a massive scale. So I think everyone now, including us

Americans, agrees that something has to be done to move from the present dangerous degree of speculative exposure to some kind of more orderly relationship between marks, franks, yen, dollars.

What is the basis to be? It seems to me there are really only three choices. As I see it, the three choices are: first, to have a series of "bloc" currency areas, rather than worldwide unrestricted exchanges. One could imagine at least three such areas: a continental American bloc, a Euro-African one, and a pan-Asian bloc. *Within* these currency blocs there would exist very easy, free exchangeability, but *between* the currency blocs there would be essentially negotiated exchange relationships—that is, fixed exchange rates. As we know from European experience, it is not easy to create such blocs, but I think it could be done if the pressure were great enough. That is one possibility.

The second possibility is once again to find a currency, or some currency unit, that will serve like the Rock of Gibraltar to which all other countries would tie their currencies. That is, of course, what Bretton Woods did, and that's where the dollar played its critical role. I don't think the dollar is likely to be able to play that role any more, because the United States has not really resolved its large position in the world economy very satisfactorily. Could it be a group of currencies that are put into a bundle and would serve as some kind of gold or goldlike Rock of Gibraltar? Possibly.

And the third possibility is gold. Gold has the extraordinary magical property of commanding belief and that's what money is, after all; it's some kind of collective psychosis in whose defense people are willing to go to extraordinary lengths. Gold serves that purpose quite well. The problem with gold is partly moral. There are a large number of people who are outraged at the idea that gold should be the center of world finance. Vergil's *auri sacra fames*, the "cursed hunger for gold," seems to be a very dubious basis on which to create the world order. Secondly, the more technical problem is that the existence of a gold standard is no guarantee that the world is going to abide by the "rules" without which gold will not bring exchange stability. Still, it is imaginable that gold might become—I underline *might* become—the basis on which this exchange stability is founded. I tend to think myself, however, that the effort will be to recreate Bretton Woods, using not just the dollar but a group of currencies linked in some formal manner to serve as the basis for exchange relationships. If that can't be achieved, my guess is that we will move toward some sort of area currency bloc system. And if everything breaks down we'll go back to gold. We'll have to wait and see.

Yes, some very interesting points. Your observation about large-scale competition. Do I understand that you are to some degree for some kind of protectionism in this respect or not?

Yes, I am. I think it's now permissible to use the word without immediately rushing to apologize for it, because as you know it's been a very bad word. And Adam Smith wrote in *The Wealth of Nations* that it was possible with a high enough tariff to grow very good grapes in Scotland, in hot houses. It would only cost thirty times as much as the wine from France. Of course, protectionism can be a most destructive and anti-progressive policy, but it is also the case that modern technology creates very destructive forms of competition. I'm thinking of the ability to create high technology, low-wage centers of production in places that are literally half way round the world, and then to send back from these Hong Kongs, and Taiwans and Singapores and Malaysias, an artillery barrage of inexpensive commodities into Houston and Berlin and Amsterdam and London. This raises problems again for the stability of the world economy and for employment prospects, which are very different from the kinds of problems that were in people's minds when the general free trade arguments were developed. I'm thinking in particular—since I am, after all, American—of the fact that there are now 100,000 to 200,000 automobile workers who will never again work in an automobile plant and probably as many steel workers who will never again work in a steel plant in the United States. And you know, they're not just scattered randomly, one automobile worker here and one steel worker there. That kind of random unemployment can easily be dealt with by general demand policies. It's 100,000 people concentrated in a few communities. I went two years ago through Pennsylvania, where the antiquated plants of some steel companies had been shut down, and found whole towns that were unemployed. That's a terrific social problem because it's very difficult to know what industries to move in, and it's difficult to know how to retrain

people to move out. People don't retrain so easily when they're thirty-
five or forty-five years old. And it then becomes a question of a
different set of premises in making the determination as to how intelligent protectionism is. Protectionism has always had one essential
premise: that the ultimate well being of an economic system is the
well-being of the *consumer*. This is really Adam Smith's argument.
The well-being of the consumer is the moral justification of the economic system. Well, that's all very well so long as it was assumed
that the well-being of producers would take care of itself. And I
think it was correctly assumed that it *would* take care of itself—
because it was imagined to be, as I said, one person unemployed
here and one person unemployed there. When unemployment assumes
the kind of massive characteristics that it has taken in the United
States, and that I think it might take elsewhere under the conditions
of modern technological competition, the balance of the argument
between protecting the well-being of producers and the well-being
of consumers changes. It's not such an open and shut matter as to
whether the well-being of America is best advanced by making available Toyotas and Hondas that are cheaper than Chevrolets or Fords,
or by protecting the livelihoods of 150,000–200,000 people. In other
words, I think that the arguments for protectionism have taken a new
turn because of the extraordinary capabilities of international
competition.

*I see. I have one closing question. On the basis of your ideas about the answers
to the questions you raised, do you foresee that the recovery will continue, or
do you see a collapse again? What is your idea about that?*

I think we are very likely to go through a period of ten or twenty
years whose principal characteristic will be the political struggle to
work to find workable political solutions for our problems. Workable
solutions for restraining inflation are a political question, not just an
economic question. Workable solutions for unemployment—again,
at heart a political question. Workable solutions for international
financial and trade relationships, and, although I haven't discussed
it, some kind of workable solutions between the rich and the poor
nations—all political problems. Now, it's not impossible to imagine
various solutions to all these matters, but they depend very much on

the outcome of domestic and political contests. They depend on whether Europe and America move to the right or to the left, whether the political climate becomes more or less ideological; more or less pragmatic; whether capitalism becomes more socialized or whether it goes in the other direction. Those are very hard things to predict. My guess is that while those political struggles take place, we are not going to have a period of great prosperity comparable to the 1950's and 1960's. But I also do not think we are going to have a period of utter collapse. I think we will live in a kind of in between world, in which we try to work our way toward a resolution of these issues. To the extent that we succeed, we may lay the basis for another long upswing—another Kondratief cycle—if they exist. My own inclinations lie in a direction of social democratic policies that will move capitalism in a "Swedish" direction. I don't know if that is possible. If not, I fear that the stage may be set for very severe internal political and economic stresses, the consequences of which we cannot really foresee.

Thank you very much.

In conclusion:

This conversation shows Professor Heilbroner, as Professor Klein, to be a very global thinker. In certain areas he argues in favor of intervention and a certain amount of planning. Especially important in this context are his comments about the necessity of protectionism at a time that economic developments in various parts of the world are so divergent that the consequences for production and employment are massive and far-reaching. Professor Heilbroner, in this regard, has a tendency to speak of a basically new situation, especially because of the modern role of technology. Others will undoubtedly think differently about this issue and hold to free unrestricted trade.

T. Charles Erickson

Professor James Tobin was born in Champaign, Illinois, in 1918. In 1981 he received the Nobel prize in Economics. He has been a Professor at Yale since 1957.

Professor Tobin is an extremely gifted theoretician, who has made fundamental contributions to economic theory. He, in particular, has expanded upon the monetary aspects of Keynes' theory, while grounding them more securely than did Keynes. Tobin specifically highlighted the significance of money in the context of economic growth. In so doing he did not limit himself to theoretical studies, but also conducted a good deal of empirical research. Tobin was a member of the Council of Economic Advisers under President Kennedy. In general, he is a proponent of a Keynesian approach to the issue of unemployment, as the risk of inflation is less significant to him than the enormous costs of production losses and unemployment.

AN INTERVIEW WITH

JAMES TOBIN

YALE

Professor Heertje: *What are your views of the present recovery, both in the United States and world-wide? Do you think it will continue or not and what are the major problems ahead?*

Professor Tobin: Are you going to ask me another question or do you just want me to start on the general. . .

I think perhaps we can restrict it to this one, but I think I would also like to ask you, because I know more or less your answer now, what your view is about the budget deficit. So if you can take that into account already, then there wouldn't be any need for me to ask another question. But if not I will bring that up.

Yes, well, you can do that. . . .

Although the recovery has started vigorously in the United States, I think one has to be skeptical about its duration and strength, both in the United States and in the rest of the world. The main reason for that is basically the fear that policy makers have concerning the resumption of inflation. In the 1970's, both of the major recoveries ended with an acceleration of inflation, and for that reason I think our policy makers, both in the United States and in other countries, are quite cautious. They fear that recovery itself will be inflationary.

Now I refer particularly to monetary policy in the United States. Fortunately, last year the Federal Reserve under Paul Volcker suspended its monetary targets, and by doing so they rescued the United States from a disastrously deep depression and probably rescued the rest of the world as well. They also averted a more severe crisis in the international debt of Third World countries. The question is whether the Federal Reserve will be prepared to accommodate, indeed to stimulate, a recovery that goes very far—that is, goes very far in terms of the reduction of unemployment, which is still extraordinarily high in the United States and all over the advanced democratic capitalist world. They will fear that reducing unemployment too much will lead to a resumption of inflation. The symptom of that in the United States is that real interest rates are still very high, historically higher than they generally have been at this phase of the business cycle. As a result of the caution of the Federal Reserve, it is quite possible that interest rates will rise further from their present levels. Then at one point or another the recovery will stall; it will lack the strength in investment by businesses and by households that is essential to keep a recovery going and to restore prosperity and higher levels of both employment and utilization of capital capacity. It's really monetary policy that is the key to the situation, and basically it's the monetary policy of the United States.

One of the principal ways in which our monetary policy brought our own economy in the United States to the deepest depression that we've had since the 1930's was by appreciating the value of the dollar in international currency markets. That's a natural response to high interest rates in a world of floating exchange rates. The higher interest rates in the United States attract funds into dollar assets and raise the value of the dollar. But that has devastated our exports. Our net export position, exports compared to imports, was one of the major factors in 1982 in the overall reduction of aggregate demand.

At the same time, high interest rates copied by other countries have made the general interest rate level quite high throughout the world. Consequently, our policy hasn't been welcome to other countries even though it's helped their trade balances.

By appreciating the dollar 40 percent in three years, we have given U.S. producers a serious handicap in world competition. An irony, a tragic irony, is that this handicap leads to protectionist pressures, which are bad enough anyway in hard times, during a depression such as we had until recently.

Now I know that many people believe that the interest rate problem is one of fiscal policy rather than monetary policy, that it is the consequence of the U.S. budget deficit. But I don't think that's true, right now, because there just hasn't been enough private demand for funds in the financial markets to be crowded out by federal borrowing. Indeed the deficits have served a useful purpose in absorbing savings that would otherwise have gone to waste in higher unemployment and lower production. Now it's possible that in the future the crowding-out problem could become important, and it's possible that some anticipation of a condition that might occur in the late 1980's is a factor in current long-term interest rates. But the Fed demonstrated last year, even when the fiscal position was looking bad, that monetary policy could lower both short and long rates. I still think monetary policy is the key to lower rates and to perpetuation of the recovery. It would be a good idea in years to come to reduce the large deficit that would remain in the federal budget in prosperous times, but we're a long way from prosperous times now. So the main problem of keeping the recovery going is having accommodative monetary policies that will lower real interest rates rather than raising them, and the danger is now.

Could I ask you one question in this respect? Your reasoning seems based mainly on the fear of inflation coming up again. Isn't it true, however, that the rate of inflation is now very low in the United States?

The rate of inflation is very low in the United States.

Secondly, the increase in the money supply figures is also rather modest at the moment, and thirdly, perhaps the productivity figures will be much better than everybody now thinks so that in the long run the rate of inflation could even be lower, too, if we take into account what is going on with technology and with the increase in productivity.

I think that at a time when we are using only three-quarters of our industrial capacity and when we have still nearly 10 percent of our labor force unemployed, we don't have to worry too much about an early resumption of inflation. I also think that concerns about it are exaggerated because they are based on an unthinking extrapolation of what happened in the two recoveries in the 1970's: one in 1973–74, when the first OPEC crisis burst upon us, and another one in 1978–79, when the second OPEC crisis and the Iranian revolution occurred.

It seems to me that those bursts of inflation were due to those events and not in any major way due to recovery in the United States itself. I don't think those things are likely to happen again in the 1980's. One thing we have successfully done is adapt to the new energy and oil prices. I don't expect that we will run into the kind of shock that led to double-digit inflation in the United States on those two occasions in the 1970's. But I know that policy makers and financial markets are very nervous about these things.

Another favorable thing for inflation—I guess the silver lining in the cloud of severe recession and depression—is that wage behavior seems much more rational than it did in the 1970's. The industries that have been most hard hit happen to be ones in which unions were very strong. Their wage gains were quite large in the past and were often taken as a pattern for other wage negotiations. Also I think productivity is very likely to revive; the slowdown of productivity growth in the late 1970's will be reversed. I think that a lot of productivity slowdown was due to the energy situation itself and to the general slack in the economy. If we do have a strong recovery, given the success we have had in adapting to the energy situation, I think productivity will snap back. That will be a help, at least in the short run, in the control of inflation, to be sure.

So, on the whole, you would be optimistic about a sustainable recovery if Volcker would be prepared to lower the rates of interest through a less restrictive monetary policy.

Yes, I would be optimistic. If it's desired to buy some insurance against the resumption of inflation, I don't think we should buy it by having several extra points of unemployment for the rest of the century, either in this country or in Europe and Japan or elsewhere in the advanced democratic capitalist world. In this country, I think we could return to having some government policy about wages and prices, some understanding between management, labor and government about guideposts; that would be a cheaper form of insurance than holding the economy stagnant in order to avoid the risk of accelerating inflation, even if, as it seems to me, that risk is not as great as is estimated by other people, including the central bank. So I think that we could go ahead and we should go ahead. After all, the purpose of the economy is to produce goods and services, and we ought to produce them.

Okay. Well, I would like to thank you very much again, Professor Tobin, and I am very grateful to you.

I would like to add one more thing. In a previous answer I assigned a great deal of responsibility for the world situation, for the recession and also for the recovery, to the United States and specifically to the U.S. central bank. We shouldn't forget that there are other locomotives in the world economy these days—Germany, the major country in the European community, and Japan—and it would be good if they also took some responsibility for the restoration of prosperity. It would have been good if the leaders at the summit conference at Williamsburg had agreed on some program to get the world out of the present stagnation, but they didn't. And I'm afraid that Germany and Japan are dragging their feet as usual; they never have learned to assume international responsibilities for the world economy commensurate to their new importance and strength. They rely instead on export stimulus as the means of prosperity in their own countries. We can't all gain by exports alone. One person's exports are somebody else's imports. So I would emphasize that these are international problems and not just to be laid on the shoulders of the United States.

In conclusion:

The main point Professor Tobin makes here is the necessity for lowering interest rates by means of a more flexible monetary policy. If interest rates do not fall, any recovery will be doomed before it can take hold. Such a reflationary policy can allow the use of production capacities so that unemployment is considerably lowered. Tobin does not share the fear of monetary authorities that inflation will rise. This is because, on the one hand, external shocks, such as oil crises, are not occurring now, and on the other, that production figures are good. He does not expect his recommendations to be followed.

Basil Blackwell

Professor Frank Hahn was born in Berlin in 1925. Currently he is a Professor at Cambridge University. He is one of the most prominent mathematical economists of our time. He has made many basic contributions to pure economic theory. In particular he has concentrated on the foundations of the theory of general balance. This theory describes a connection between the behavior of all consumers and producers functioning within an economy. It is noteworthy that of all those interviewed, Professor Hahn demonstrated, in his answer to the question about the future of the world economy, the strongest tendency towards finding clues within economic theory.

AN INTERVIEW WITH

FRANK HAHN

CAMBRIDGE

Professor Heertje: *Professor Hahn, I would like to ask you the same question as I have put to your colleagues about the prospects of the present recovery, either worldwide or just in the United States and England—I leave it to you to choose. What are you views about that? Do you think that we will run across the same kinds of problems we have experienced in the past?*

Professor Hahn: Well, I think economists shouldn't be soothsayers. Our discipline is quite good at understanding particular situations but, contrary to Milton Friedman's view, it is not very good at predicting. Many people have predicted things that never occurred. Or the opposite occurred. So we are very careful in predicting anything about the current recovery. Perhaps the best way of starting to answer your question is to say that if one believes what seems to be the theory at least of the advisers of President Reagan and Mrs. Thatcher, and others elsewhere, a recovery is extremely unlikely. The argument goes something as follows: we cannot pursue Keynesian policies because if we did we would cause inflation and not recovery. Workers are, moreover, unwilling to face a reduction in real wages, required in order to get employment higher, in the short run at least.

Let us suppose that the economy starts recovering without the aid of government Keynesian policies. That would mean, I suppose that firms would become more optimistic about the future, investment would pick up, production would pick up. The question is whether that would allow the elán to continue without an upward pressure on prices and money wages. I say there would be a substantial increase, actually, in pressure on prices and wages, in particular since the recovery is not likely to be coordinated between countries. If Britain were to start recovering at all reasonably now, for instance, this would put considerable pressure on our exchange rate, and that in itself would raise prices and therefore wages. Now when prices and wages rise, if you combine that with a tight monetary policy, then you kill the recovery in its infancy. And I think there are considerable signs that this is what is happening. For instance, in America, where there were signs of recovery a few months ago, or half a year ago, there's been a considerable dispute between the Fed and the Reagan government on monetary control, and it looks at the moment as if the resistance to high interest rates has been successful, but it's doubtful that it will last, especially with the large budget deficit they have. And if you then have a tight monetary policy, you are likely to kill the recovery. My own feeling is, and I want to put that perhaps differently from those of the others you have interviewed, is that the real problem of the last part of the century is not to cure inflation but to learn to live with inflation. As long as we make the control of inflation top priority, we will not see any substantial recovery. I think that the process, what's happened really is that there's been a considerable social change in all the Western economies. Historians always talk about the rise of the middle classes in the eighteenth and nineteenth centuries and the industrial revolution and the growth of capitalism. Well, our century is the century of the rise of the working classes and we don't have any institutions to deal with this. The outward sign of the growing power of the working class is inflation. Instead of leaning against the wind, we ought to live with inflation.

Here is a point that is totally misunderstood throughout the world. It you took Professor Friedman and the monetarists' views seriously, inflation would hardly matter at all. If there is a 10 percent rise in prices each year and money wages rise 10 percent and if taxes are indexed, the cost of inflation to the society is very small indeed. Now, of course, you mustn't have runaway inflation, because that would ruin a monetary economy, but to live with the idea of bringing down inflation and to look at every rise in prices as a disaster is, I think, a social disaster. And I would like to say most categorically that there is no economic theory at present, anywhere in the world, whether monetarist, Keynesian, or anything else, that can find any substantial real costs of inflation once that inflation has been adapted to—that's to say, once people have anticipated it more or less correctly and the government has indexed taxes.

I have one question in respect to the relationship between inflation and the rate of interest, both the nominal and the real rate of interest. If you bring down inflation, wouldn't you also bring down the rate of interest and therefore stimulate investment?

No, I don't think that is true. I do not agree with that. In fact, during our highest inflation, certainly in America and England, I don't know whether in Holland, the real rate of interest—that is to say, the nominal rate of interest minus the expected rate of inflation—was negative. It is now extremely positive. In other words, bringing down the inflation rate has produced a very high positive real rate of interest. Now the interesting thing is that the negative real rate of interest did not stimulate a great deal of investment. In fact, the reverse: it was associated with falling investment. So the stimulus of interest rates on investment is very dubious. If we have inflation, nominal interest rates would be higher.

In pure theory, the inflation rate would have no effect whatsoever on the real rate of interest, none at all. In fact, if anything, it should bring it down. Let us suppose that you start with zero inflation, that people hold a certain amount of money for convenience and financial assets, and that they hold also real assets, amongst which I want to include shares on the stock exchange. Now suppose inflation rises from zero to 10 percent. Then if you hold a guilder, it falls in real value by 10 percent per annum, so that you will have an incentive to move out of money into real assets. In particular, you have an incentive to lend money to people who are going to use it to buy machines and to produce goods, which are indexed to some extent because prices are rising. So in fact the real rate of interest is likely to fall with inflation. An important point I want to make here is that recent research has indicated that we don't really fully understand the investment process. For ages economists thought that the price of a loan was an important element in investment decisions. It turns out, both theoretically and otherwise, that there's a lot of credit rationing. In fact, for theoretical reasons, we would expect there to be credit rationing, and that is due to the fact that the lender isn't clear how safe his loan is. That is to say, he doesn't know the risk of bankruptcy of the borrower. Now let us suppose that when there is a greater demand for loans, he simply raises the rate of interest. What will happen? The class of borrowers who are willing to take large, unreliable risks are going to stay, and the safer borrowers will leave. That's called the "theory of adverse selection." In other words, if you ration credit by price, there will be a tendency to adversely select the more risky enterprises. What has therefore happened is that people ration credit. When you go into a bank, they don't say, all right you can borrow as much as you like at x percent, they say, how much can you borrow at x percent? Now credit rationing is far more important, in my view, than the rate of interest, although I don't deny that people with fixed interest obligations may have cash flow problems when interest rates rise. I don't deny that.

Could we bring into the picture one other element, the fact that in a certain period there may be or there may not be a whole set of new technical possibilities, methods of production, and also new possibilities as to new products? I cannot avoid the idea that at this moment, for example, in the United States, there is a lot of new technology available that is waiting to be applied and a strong tendency to invest, even with the very high real rate of interest.

Yes, I quite agree. In textbook economics we distinguish between investment more or less in the same sort of things because demand has gone up—I think it may have been Keynes who called this "widening" investment; "deepening" investment because the relative prices of capital goods and labor have changed and you want to use more capital per man; third, what you are now mentioning, which is very important, investment simply because of new technology, new products, innovations in general. Now, there's no doubt, I think, that there is a kind of, I don't want to call it revolution, but there's a lot of new technical know-how developing from robots to electronics of all kinds, and there's very little doubt that that's going to stimulate

investment on its own in some way. On the other hand, certainly, it
is not independent of demand. That is to say, a deep recession is not
always a good time to start on this sort of innovative investment,
although it ought to be said that the very famous economist Joseph
Schumpeter argued that that is the way recessions and depressions
end—that eventually when old capital has not been maintained, the
profitability of new investments increases even though demand is
relatively low. Now it is, of course, possible that that is the way our
recovery will come about. The more it comes about this way, of
course, the more likely it is to persist, at least for some time, because
it would then allow real wages to rise even though employment is
rising. But the impression one gains is that in the new recovery, if
it's led by innovations, there will be relatively small effect on employment, because the new technology seems to be peculiarly labor-saving. But to decide whether technology is labor-saving or not requires
rather sophisticated analysis. You can't just go and look and say, ah,
you can now produce motor cars with robots. You have to ask your-
self how the robots are produced and how the things that produced
the robots are produced and so on and so forth. It's a complicated
story, but the impression generally is that the capital-labor ratio, if
you like, is going to be higher. Now the higher the capital-labor ratio
is, the higher the level of income has to be in order to get a given
level of employment. That's just arithmetic. And it's the part of the
story I'm not at all optimistic about. I think that we may have a
recovery in GNP perhaps, led by these innovations, but I don't think
we'll have the same kind of recovery in employment.

But isn't reduction of labor time a normal effect of using advanced technology?

That is a very good question. I mean, reduction of labor time is
equivalent to a rise in real wages. If you look at the history of hours
of work—and I'm afraid by history I mean British history, because
I don't know any other—the extraordinary thing is that on every
single occasion I know of, hours of work were reduced either by act
of parliament or by some other public action, such as the unions
getting together with the employers. Hours of work don't seem to
be reducible by the market. In fact, hours of work are a little in the
nature of what economists call a "public good." And the reason is, I

think, that if your factory works eight hours a day and another factory works five hours a day, then communication between the two
is dead for three hours. That is to say, hours of work are interrelated.
It's what we call an externality. There are other explanations that
derive from the theory of games, but I don't think I want to go into
that. If that's true, then hours of work are things that in some sense
have to be done collectively, changed collectively.

The difficulties of changing collectively are quite considerable
because it's clear that a man would prefer to work six hours instead
of eight hours a day, but it's not clear how much of his wages he's
willing to give up in exhange. To reduce the hours of work without
a reduction in real wages, therefore, we need to have substantial
technological progress. Moreover, if I'm right in saying hours of work
are a collective good, there are going to be difficulties, because technical progress is not going to be universal across all industries. If you
change them collectively, some industries will therefore get into serious trouble. But I agree with you that that is the likely outcome—
in fact, that it must be our hope. Civilization seems to me to progress
by people spending less time in unpleasant work and more time
enjoying work.

*So, if there isn't a recovery as a result of technical change, by innovation,
you would be rather pessimistic as to the present situation?*

Yes, but I am not pessimistic on the grounds that I can make a forecast
of what will happen. I am pessimistic because I feel there are very
grave doubts whether recovery can be brought about using economic
theory—and by that I mean any particular school. The process may
each time be choked off in its infancy because of the tremendous
preoccupation with inflation. People now think of inflation as a sin.
If you ask, let us say, Mrs. Thatcher, why it is bad to kill, she will
probably say, because it is morally wrong. And that seems to me a
reasonable answer. If you ask Mrs. Thatcher why inflation is bad,
she would say, because it is bad. There's no reason. Now, we're
interested in the welfare of the citizens of a country, and the idea
that inflation is evil in itself seems to me a very silly way of arguing.
It's not that inflation is evil in itself, it is that inflation causes the
welfare of the people to decline. This has nothing to do with eco-

nomics. Somehow or other people lose confidence in the stability of
their governments when there's inflation. The stability of their currency is somehow linked in people's minds with the stability of their
political and social institutions. There are historical reasons for that—
for instance, the runaway inflations in Germany in the twenties, in
Hungary, and all that sort of thing.

And now in Israel.

And now in Israel. Israel is a very good example. I mean, I'd like to
put that in; I have visited Israel on three occasions, the last when the
inflation rate I think was 110 percent. I was very widely entertained,
I met a large number of people, not just economists, and at not a
single occasion can I remember the conversation turning to inflation.
Nobody seemed to worry about it. That's not quite true, of course.
Some of those people, if you ask them outright, would much prefer
to have it lower, but the fact is that it was not a burning issue. Now
Israel is exceptional because they have so many other burning issues
that this may be pushed into the background.

And everything has been indexed as to price.

And everything has been indexed. This is a very important point,
because it is attitudes to inflation that are going to ruin the recovery
in my view. Let us suppose that when Mrs. Thatcher was elected in
1979, holding exactly the views she holds, instead of saying, we will
bring inflation down, she had said, we will stabilize it at 20 percent.
Mrs. Thatcher and her advisors believe that inflation is entirely con-
trollable by the behavior of monetary aggregates, and there's nothing
special about the number zero. Zero inflation is no better than 20
percent, though if all prices went up by 20 percent each year, there
would be a small increase in uncertainty because not all prices would
rise simultaneously and there would be a certain distortion of relative
prices.

I've put this point to Mrs. Thatcher's advisor, Professor Sir Allen
Walters. He gave me a most remarkable reply. He said, of course
you're right, it isn't the inflation that matters, it's the variability of
inflation that matters. But who's responsible for the variability of

inflation according to their theory? The monetary authorities. So if it's only the variability that matters, then what she should have done is to say, well, you must not have variability in the monetary aggregates; we will stabilize them first to maintain the present inflation rate. There would not have been runaway inflation on their own theory. People would have adjusted to it, and we wouldn't have had to go through the trauma of trying to reduce inflation. Because reducing inflation is bound by everybody's account to reduce real output. And it would be very useful if the citizens of Western Europe, or the Western world, including America perhaps, added up the cost in goods foregone in fighting inflation over the past three years. It's astronomical . . . astronomical. They ought to compare it with the benefits of now saying that prices only rise by 6 percent instead of 20 percent.

That's a very interesting point, especially from the point of theory, but isn't the practical experience that if you, say, start with 2 percent inflation a year, it can easily go to 4 percent? Still, you say it's not too bad, but then it moves up to 6 and 8 percent.

Well, I think it does. I think there I have a certain amount of sympathy with the monetarists, because this comes back to what I said about the rise of the working classes. I do think that the government should have targets, probably both in expenditure and in monetary aggregates. My argument is that it's a mistake to try and bring inflation down. Moreover, I think the target should be a realistic one, because, you see, if you argue that you can control inflation or bring it down to zero by controlling the monetary aggregate, then you ought to agree that you can control and keep it at 2 percent or 5 percent by controlling the monetary aggregate. In other words, I think there needs to be some kind of monetary discipline, largely because you have to somehow or other deal with runaway wage problems. There are, of course, people in England who argue that our unemployment was not unexpected but designed, that Mrs. Thatcher's policies—and probably Reagan's, but let's stick to Mrs. Thatcher—have nothing whatsoever to do with monetarism but are designed to discipline the working classes. In that she has undoubtedly succeeded. The real question is, has she broken them once and for all in some sense. In which case, I ought to admit, recovery is more likely actually, given the other views they hold. Or will the power of the unions come back again at the first sign of upturn?

I remember that in another connection Lawrence Klein made more or less the same point about Reagan's policy with respect to the air traffic controllers, and that that was a very essential point in his policy, much more important than a monetarist approach and things like that, because there he made it clear he was very strong.

I am sort of left of center, but I do think that British trade union power was getting out of hand. You know, there is a saying in English, power without responsibility is the prerogative of the whore. And that's what they had. It wasn't so much that they caused inflation as that they simply put a spanner in almost every piece of technical progress we had. I mean, it really had become intolerable. So, if Mrs. Thatcher's policies, if that interpretation of her policies is at all correct, and if she has succeeded in it, then I have to admit the prospects of recovery would be better.

Okay, I think we should leave it at that. Thank you very much.

In conclusion:

Professor Hahn takes a somber view of the chance for recovery in the world economy if one stubbornly sticks to fighting inflation by all possible means. He judges the cost for this policy to be enormously high. Only if it becomes truly possible to contain the power of employees for the time being, is recovery in the long term a possibility despite a low rate of inflation. A certain degree of inflation must inevitably be accepted as employees regain their strong influence. If this does not happen, economic development stagnates, and production losses will result.

Born in 1918 at Uman, Kiev, Russia, John Marion Letiche is Professor of Economics at the University of California, Berkeley. His field is international economics. He has been a Guggenheim Fellow and the recipient from the University of Verona of the Adam Smith Medal. He has served as economic advisor to the U.N. as well as to the U.S.A. Departments of State, Treasury, Labor, and HUD, and also to the President's Council of Economic Advisors. He has written or edited more than ten books, while contributing in several languages to major journals of economics.

AN INTERVIEW WITH
JOHN M. LETICHE

CALIFORNIA

Professor Heertje: *Well, as you know, we have spoken with several well-known economists about the perspectives of the world economy, whether there will be a recovery or not, and we also went into the question of what kinds of problems we may foresee in the future if it turns out that there will be a recovery. Will we run into the problem of inflation again or not, and things like that. We would very much like to have your views about these kinds of questions and your interpretation of what has been said by the others.*

Professor Letiche: The situation at the moment is extremely interesting and difficult, because the outlook I have encountered among the British government officials with respect to the UK economic recovery and the general view I have found among European leaders is, in my judgment, one of excessive pessimism. On the other side, in the United States, the recovery is going along satisfactorily, but there is the view among many in America that the recovery there is accelerating much too fast. I find these positions to be extremes not warranted by the evidence. For example, your listeners have heard Professor Friedman claim that there are only two possible outcomes for the current situation. One is that the Federal Reserve System in the United States will so expand the quantity of money that we will be back into double-digit inflation in the next few years. The other possibility is that, because the quantity of money has been rising too rapidly in the United States during 1981–82 (and even more recently), the chairman of the Federal Reserve, Mr. Volcker, and the Board of Governors will step on the brakes too quickly, the quantity of money will be reduced, rates of interest will again rise appreciably, and the American economic expansion will be aborted—in other words, the recovery will be brought to a halt by mid-1984.

Let me state at once that as I look at the record and at the current tempo of the U.S. and Western European economic activity, I think the evidence does not lead to these conclusions. In fact, the recovery that is now going on in the United States is probably about right if we take into consideration the depths to which the economy had fallen. The economic expansion during the past few months has been taking place at the high rate of 8 or 9 percent on an annual basis; this, however, will not last long. Beginning from such a low level of recession, it is not unusual for the United States to experience rapid rates of growth in the early stages of recovery. If one has to risk making a moderate mistake, I think it is better to do so on the side of a somewhat more rapid expansion that will reduce the high unemployment rate a little faster rather than risk falling back and continuing the recession for a still longer period of time. The data show that in the United States sales to consumers have been quite broadly based: in housing, cars, furniture—in most industries. The available evidence also shows that the recovery is slowly beginning to take place in private capital investment. For the expansion to be robust and firm, it must, of course, move into the investment areas, and that is now occurring.

Consequently, I believe that the two extreme alternatives that Professor Friedman presented are not the most likely ones. I believe that for the next few years, say from 1983 to 1986, the American economy can well expand between 3 and 4 percent a year. One of the most important things that has recently happened in the United States is that labor and management do not expect inflation to be quickly and precipitously triggered again. Professor Tobin was correct in stating that the atmosphere has been substantially stabilized, and that the labor markets in the United States are working quite well. If the monetary aggregates expand at the moderate rates to which the Federal Reserve is now committed, I think there is a good possibility that the tremendous innovations that are occurring in the United

States—in many branches of the communications industry, in micro processing, in bio-engineering, in health care delivery systems—will prove to be as important as any previous innovative expansions.

In Europe, however, I find the situation disturbing and serious. For example, in the United Kingdom, expectations were engendered before the recent election that the rate of economic expansion would be faster than it has in fact been. The evidence appears to show that Great Britain has become more closely tied to the European Economic Community than to the United States. This position has recently been emphasized to me by many British economists. The expansion in America, it is therefore argued, may not give as much economic leverage either to the United Kingdom or to the entire European Economic Community as it did in the past. Although consumer expenditures in Britain have been rising rapidly, the percentage of income saved has sharply declined. As compared with a more normal trend, people have been using savings for their increased expenditures, and now the government finds that capital investment has not grown as rapidly as it had anticipated. The most recent evidence on the growth of real private fixed investment has been very disappointing. Consumer sales in the domestic market have also grown relative to exports. Growth of real domestic product was recently rising at about 2 percent a year, but for the near future it is expected to rise at a somewhat lower rate. British officials are therefore pessimistic. I gained the impression of increased economic vitality, however, and with a record of recent increases in productivity, I believe that, in the medium term, the tempo of economic expansion in Britain will rise.

The current German economic situation is also cause for pessimism, although a revival appears to have begun. Unfortunately, in practically all European countries, as well as in the United States, the required change in the structural side of the budgets has not taken place on a sufficient scale. Even in Japan, the structural budget deficit has been rising rapidly. Profits have been low, and real wages have been inflexible downwards in Britain, France, Germany, and even Japan. In Western Europe, the incentives for a substantial expansion of private capital investment have, therefore, not as yet developed. But I believe the current economic expansion in the United States, with rapidly rising productivity and profits in many indus-

tries, will help Western European economies to a greater extent than
is now envisaged.

The overvalued dollar, in my estimation an overvaluation of between
20 and 25 percent, will mean that as the U.S. economy grows more
quickly than the European economies, the latter will gain some leverage. The evidence already shows that American imports are expanding much more rapidly than exports, and the United States is moving
toward a deficit on current account. That is important and beneficial
both for the European economies and the developing nations. But it
is not an unmixed blessing. The U.S. government tends to emphasize the positive aspects of this development; namely, that the overvalued dollar will help the European nations to expand their exports
to the United States and this will accelerate their growth rates. When
Western European countries export more goods to the United States
than they import from it, this means that their domestic investment
is smaller than their savings. In the short term, at least, this would
tend to lower the growth rate of European per capita levels of consumption. As one of the richest countries in the world, the United
States would not necessarily well serve the economic interests of
Europe by being a net absorber of resources. I think it is important
that the overvalued dollar gradually begin to decline relative to key
European currencies. This would more satisfactorily be brought about
if we had more consultation and cooperation in monetary policy,
exchange rate policy, and budgetary policy among the governments
of the United States, the European Economic Community, and Japan.
There has in fact been some retrogression in this regard. One thing
the previous people interviewed have not stressed is that the U.S.
monetary policies, budgetary policies, exchange-rate policies, and
alleged freer trade policies have not been consistent with one another.
Unfortunately, the budget deficit of the United States has recently
been so large, and avowed policy regarding it so erratic, that it has
not permitted a stable monetary policy. Professor Friedman was right
in stating that the monetary policy of the United States has been
extremely volatile. It has not been monetarist, although many government officials have used the rhetoric of monetarism. In many
important industries, the volatility of interest rates did not operate
to bring about effective adjustments but caused them to stagnate.
Western European countries faced the alternatives of either seeing

similar rises in their interest rates or attempting to stabilize them and experiencing large capital outflows to the United States. In either case, the extreme volatility of interest rates and/or exchange rates increased selective protectionism: in America the onslaught of the recession, combined with the overvalued dollar, enhanced the pressures for protectionism; in Europe the recession, with extraordinarily high rates of unemployment, had a similar effect; and in Japan, which kept its interest rates at lower levels, capital flight to the United States so lowered the value of the yen that both the United States and Western European countries imposed restrictions against imports. It is in these respects that volatile budget deficits, monetary policies, and exchange rates became inconsistent not only with one another but with freer trade policies. Now European exporters fear that a substantial rise in their exports to the United States may be met by ad hoc increases in protectionism through national administrative "fair trade" procedures rather than through the more demanding GATT "unfair trade" provisions. In too many cases, both in Europe and America, industries have been devising industrial policies through disguised corruption of their commercial obligations under the GATT rules. Although it is my view that the world economy has reasonably good growth prospects for the next three or four years, and it is not as pessimistic as other people have been, we will urgently need more responsible leadership and behavior from the main countries in the world.

What has struck me so far is the fact that you say that the dollar is overvalued at the moment and even give a figure, saying that it is overvalued by 20 to 25 percent. Could you elaborate a little bit on that? In what sense do you think the dollar is overvalued, and how is it possible to give such an exact figure?

That's an important issue. My estimate is based on the real effective exchange rate—that is, a weighted average exchange rate corrected for inflation differentials. In strict technical terms, there is no single "equilibrium exchange rate"; but if we accept purchasing-power parities as a proxy for longer-term equilibrium exchange rates—which is in accordance with the most recent econometric research—between 1980 and 1983:Q_3, the dollar became overvalued by 20 to 25 percent.

There are, of course, difficult technical issues involved. In the first half of 1983, even though U.S. imports have been rising relative to exports, the dollar has strengthened rather than weakened. According to the best available estimates, the effective dollar exchange rate will rise by approximately 10 percent on average for 1983. As the U.S. economy expands more rapidly than those in Western Europe, we would expect an increase of its demand for most European currencies, and a rise in their value relative to the dollar. But, as yet, that has not come about. It has not because the United States is the most stable political-economic country in the world. When a crisis occurs, say in the Middle East or in U.S.-Soviet relations, short-term capital in particular tends to move to the United States. I expect these instabilities to continue, and therefore do not expect the value of the dollar to decline quickly. Although the dollar is overvalued in terms of purchasing-power parities, speculative capital movements probably will continue to play an important role in the valuations of key currencies. While I believe important economic forces are now working toward equilibration of international accounts, the dollar may remain overvalued for a considerable period of time.

Professor Letiche, inasmuch as you are an expert in the field of international economics, international finance, and so on, I would like to ask what your view is of our present international exchange system. Do you foresee that there will be a major change? For example, Professor Friedman says that he thinks we will have to live with the system we have now, but others predict that there will be major changes in the future. There is also the question of the role of gold. Could you comment on this?

In so far as the exchange-rate system is concerned I think it is a serious exaggeration to argue—as Professor Friedman has done—that the floating exchange-rate system has worked "extremely well." Had he said "well," it would have been enough: during the period of floating, we have had periodic surges and declines in the values of key currencies—such as the pound and the yen—that were primarily related to disorderly, speculative, short-term capital movements. What we need is a stable exchange-rate *system*, but not stable exchange rates or freely floating exchange rates. If exchange rates remain rigid, this would definitely impede the kind of adjustments that are economically required. But floating exchange rates have been accompanied by overshooting in relative values of currencies out of all proportion to underlying economic fundamentals such as the relative purchasing-power parities of these currencies. Studies of the International Monetary Fund have shown that under current conditions intervention has worked quite successfully. I believe that a greater amount of consultation and cooperation between the main central banks is indispensable to make our exchange-rate system less volatile than it has recently been. If that is not achieved, we enhance the probability of getting the worst characteristics of both rigid exchange rates and volatile ones: for governments are then inclined individually to manage their exchange rates in terms of discriminatory national interests, with periodic large and disturbing adjustments in the relative values of important currencies. On this issue, therefore, I fundamentally disagree with Professor Friedman.

I agree with him, however, that we cannot now get agreement concerning the particular kind of exchange-rate system that the International Monetary Fund, in consultation with experts, might wish to achieve. World conditions are not propitious for agreement on a universal system. Economic analysis suggests that it is appropriate for different countries to use different devices. We have achieved important gains in the operation of the International Monetary System, and these gains have been related to some of the achievements of the International Monetary Fund. These, Professor Heertje, are some of the issues to which your question applies: is there a substantial probability that the International Monetary System will break down because of the various causes for its current instability? I believe it will not. The substantial increase of exchange-rate flexibility under the rules and surveillance of the IMF has been an important positive achievement. The prevention of a crunch in international liquidity has been another advance of primary magnitude. Here, too, the operations of the International Monetary Fund have been extremely important. An important lesson that the economics profession has learned, and that all econometric models confirm, is that despite the serious recessions we have recently had, such as the ones in 1973–75 and in 1980–82, the Western international economic system— even under great stress—remains much more stable than it ever has been before. The possibility of an international financial crash like that of the 1930s occurring in the foreseeable future must be considered practically nonexistent. I think the exchange-rate system will remain operating pretty much as it has been recently, with greater flexibility.

One recent development, however, will probably be strengthened. Because some of the important less developed countries have become terribly overcommitted, and confidence in the longer-term revival of their economies will need to be restored, the International Monetary Fund, in conjunction with the major central and commercial banks, will have to play a larger role in the restructuring of their foreign debts and in the stabilization of their economies. Argentina, Brazil, and Mexico are badly in arrears. They will be unable to meet their interest payments on foreign debt, and it will be very important that the International Monetary Fund be provided with greater resources, primarily in the form of increased quotas, to deal with crises that are bound to recur. As the international economy has grown in inter-dependence, the periodic solution of such crises—in the field of exchange rates, balance of payments, foreign debts, and restoration of monetary stability—has become increasingly a matter of multi-national interest and responsibility.

Insofar as gold is concerned, I would advise your listeners, especially those who are averse to risks, not to speculate in this asset. The price of gold fluctuates widely as a result of political crises. If expectations persist that the rates of inflation in the major countries will continue to decline, the price of gold can be expected to fall; and conversely. With South Africa and the Soviet Union being two major suppliers of gold, their periodic actions with respect to its rise or fall in supply could have a substantial effect on its price. Gold has very little significance to the operation of the current international monetary system, and I do not believe that it will have greater significance in the future. But the volatility in its price will continue. This not-withstanding, or because of it, gold will play only a very minor role in the international monetary system of the future. I wonder if you would agree with these views, Professor Heertje?

Well, I think the answer depends a little bit on your answer to my closing question, and that is: What are the chances of closer cooperation between the central banks of the major countries and the coordination of their economic policies?

That's a very profound issue. In my recent discussions with govern-ment officials—both in the United States and Western Europe—the most important impression they have made on me is that while they have not been as successful as they had hoped to be in their budgetary and monetary policies over the past few years, they seem to be on a more even keel. The lesson has been learned that with increasing rates of inflation, rates of unemployment begin to rise rather than fall. In technical terms, at least for some countries and at times, the Phillips Curve did not apply on the way up: higher rates of wage and price increase ultimately resulted in higher rates of unemployment. But it worked on the way down: it took extremely high rates of unemployment to bring inflation rates down. That is a very important lesson we have all learned. The cost for "ending" inflation has been extremely high. Consequently, every government in the developed countries will probably be taking, or will at least endeavor to take, more responsible measures in budget policy and monetary policy to try to reduce the rate of unemployment without refueling inflation. To the extent that they are successful, it will enable the central banks to cooperate more. Will that cooperation be very extensive? No, because treasuries even find it difficult to cooperate effectively with the central banks in their own countries. One of the greatest difficulties is to achieve a greater degree of consistency and integration between treasuries and central banks. Nevertheless, I think the time is long overdue to increase that cooperation both nationally and multinationally. It is occurring, slowly and quietly, and I think it should occur to a greater degree.

Okay, thank you very much.

In conclusion:

Professor Letiche is optimistic about the recovery of the world economy, especially in view of developments in the United States. He, nevertheless, emphasizes the necessity for more international coordination in the areas of monetary, exchange rate, and budgetary policies. Striking, furthermore, is his plea for a greater consistency of policy by the Central Banks and the Departments of Finance. In this regard, the issue is not only one of more cooperation on a national level, but specifically of coordination in an international context. Professor Letiche expects this to induce a more balanced development, for example, of the interest rates in the United States and Europe, and of variations in exchange rates.

Born in 1903 in The Hague, Professor Dr. Jan Tinbergen is without doubt the most famous and important Dutch economist. In 1969, he was the first recipient of the Nobel prize for Economics, along with the Norwegian, Ragnar Frisch, for his pioneering work on the dynamics of economic theory. Professor Tinbergen studied physics in Leiden, where he received his doctorate in 1929. His thesis at that time already indicated an interest in economics. During the thirties, the League of Nations commissioned him to test statistically the well-known cyclical economic theories. Afterwards he researched diverse aspects of economics, always keeping the social significance of theory in close perspective. He, thus, laid the foundation for the work of the Central Planning Bureau to follow. He gained further notoriety with his work on developing countries. The publications by Professor Tinbergen are too numerous to mention here.

AN INTERVIEW WITH

JAN TINBERGEN

ROTTERDAM

Professor Heertje: *Could you give your opinion on the development of the world economy in the coming years? Will the economic recovery continue, and what problems do you foresee?*

Professor Tinbergen: I always find it very difficult to give forecasts. I would rather limit myself to matters of policy than be forced to offer a detailed vision of the future. I'm not an expert at that, so that I'd especially like to talk about what should be done according to my own view. I consider the most important question for western countries to be high unemployment, and in a certain sense that is, of course, also the case in the Third World, where poverty, sometimes in the form of unemployment, and sometimes other forms, remains, nonetheless, one of the greatest problems in the world. One of the most important aspects in connection with that seems to me that the Brandt Commission has, quite correctly, stated that we have a common interest in getting out of this misery. I would like to emphasize that.

If we followed the recommendations of the Brandt report, it would not only help to diminish the difficulties of the Third World, but would be very significant for us, too. The simplest way to say it is that when, indeed, more funds are made available to the Third World, a significant amount comes back to us almost immediately, leading to increased orders in, for example, the metal processing industry. I'm also thinking about other branches of industry in which we have competitive power. In this context I'm thinking of electronics, for example. In this connection, I'm really not much afraid of further inflation. That is actually the often-heard counter argument: transferring larger amounts to the Third World will have to happen mainly by bringing more money into circulation—as has already been done recently by the International Monetary Fund—and that would, in turn, bring about the danger of a new wave of inflation. I don't believe much in that, and, furthermore, there are means to prevent it. I'm of the opinion that this new money would have to be withdrawn from circulation when the economy showed contined improvement. Aside from this, we always have the possibility of a so-called incomes policy. I know, of course, that this is unpopular with many, and so nowadays I sometimes use the expression "indicative" incomes policy. This means that when social partners have enough sense to reach agreements that are not inflationary (which do not lead to price increases), the government can remain uninvolved, but when an understanding is not there, the government should maintain the right to set limits, eventually, to what can happen with incomes. I say incomes on purpose, and not only wages, because such a policy, I think, should not only pertain to wages, but certainly also to the salaries and incomes of professionals.

When you say that you're not anxious about inflation caused by transferring monies from the West to, for example, developing nations, would that attitude be the same if Western Europe implemented a coordinated growth policy?

I am, indeed, much in favor of the idea of everyone undertaking something together in Europe, and as far as that's concerned, the labor unions especially are on the right track now. Not only because the FNV [Federatie van Nederlandse Vakbonden, an organization of unions] now is advocating a growth policy (as is the Labor Party, by the way), but aside from that they have already taken several steps to bring about European involvement. I just received a brochure they published about the cooperation that already exists between the Scandinavian and the German unions, and, from what I understand from the accompanying letter, they are now trying to make this a reality on the level of the EEC as well. I find it, indeed, very desirable and am in complete agreement with what the unions advocate in this regard; that, in fact, something has to take place on a supra-national level. You could say that if one country tried it, it would be very difficult. There would be an immediate retaliation with respect to the balance of payments, which would, of course, turn against that country. But if we arrived at cooperation of the ten European countries, that danger would be greatly diminished. That, in my opinion, is one of the mistakes that have been made in the past: not nearly enough attention was paid to the European Community as a potential initiator.

I think that others will object that danger threatens in these large financing deficits and that a possible consequence of this could be the increase, instead of decrease, of interest rates, plus perhaps the danger of rising inflation. How do you see that?

As far as these matters are concerned, every remark has a grain of truth to it, of course, but we must set priorities. I think decreasing unemployment is, by far, the highest priority. I'm somewhat less concerned about the budget deficits continuing to increase, although in the long run this must, of course, not be allowed to continue. I believe that in the meantime we are on our way to solving that problem because the budget deficit is largely a consequence of the huge amounts that have to be spent on unemployment benefits, for example. When we really succeed in bringing about an economic recovery, certain tendencies will come to our aid, i.e., the budgets will not remain in as precarious a position as they are now. In addition to that, as I briefly mentioned before, the budget deficit does not have to add exclusively to the increase of expenditures in the usual way, but on a worldwide scale, with the creation of money, particularly by the International Monetary Fund, some of what is necessary can be done. In connection with this, I'm thinking of the fact that the so-called Special Drawing Rights can be expanded and immediately made available for use by the International Development Association, the institution of the World Bank group that transfers money under favorable conditions to developing nations. I just read a couple of essays by Dr. H.J. Witteveen, which, to my delight, also pointed in that direction to a certain extent. He points, for example, to the fact that the volume of funds at the disposal of the IMF have been greatly lagging behind the development of world trade. This comment seems to me of great importance, because it contains an argument opposing those who are so afraid to increase the quotas of the IMF further. The latter have, of course, already been increased recently, but the Brandt Commission is asking to more than double those increases. To be precise, they have been increased 47 percent and the Brandt Commission, in its latest report, asked for an increase of 100 percent; that is, indeed, a little more than double.

Dr. Witteveen's comment that the volume of the IMF's resources are lagging behind world trade, is an important argument for following the recommendation of the Brandt Commission. It reminds me a little of an argument pertaining to the degree of integration within the European Community. I have made a comparison between the federal budget of the United States and the budget of the European Community. It just so happens that the total income of the United States and that of the ten countries of the European Community are about the same, while the federal budget of the United States, without military expenditures, is already more than ten times as big as the budget of the European Community. Those who continue to repeat that we cannot expand the means the European Community have, in my opinion, little chance of being right, for everything seems to indicate that we are not nearly integrated enough; in other words, that many more tasks should be transferred from the national to the European level. Specifically which tasks these should be, is, of course, worth examining, and I have therefore advised that we take a look at what is being done in the United States on the federal level, and not in Europe. We could draw certain conclusions from that. Furthermore, a number of our own ministers have pointed out the desirability of handling certain matters on a European level. I'm thinking, for example, of the question of a policy to stimulate industrial development. Minister van Aardenne has stated quite clearly that he is of the opinion that it should be done on a European level. There are other items that could be mentioned. Closely related to what I've just said, for example, is scientific research, which should undoubtedly be partially coordinated and financed on a European level. It is quite possible this would lead to savings for Europe as a whole by

taking a number of tasks out of the hands of national governments.
In the area of research and development there is quite a bit of dupli-
cation of effort. Also here there's an argument toward: Let's please
do more on the European level.

*I would like to return to the matter of fighting unemployment. The proponents
of an alternative policy possibly attach a very high priority to lowering
unemployment. They do advocate, however, another approach and, therefore,
I would like to return for a moment to the issue of interest rates, because policy
in regard to interest rates has played an important role in other interviews,
too. Do you see it as relatively less important whether interest rates decrease
or not because of policy?*

No, I don't want to say that, though I must confess, that I am less
at home in this area. I do, however, have an argument or two, indeed,
to attach less importance to the matter of interest rates. The work I
did at the time for the League of Nations showed me that the influence of interest rates on investments is not that great. Now, that was
long ago, at a time different from the present. Therefore, I do not
want to attach any overblown importance to it, but I do wonder if
those who emphasize this aspect so strongly are right in doing so.
Nevertheless, I am in favor of bringing interest rates, which have
been abnormal, back to more normal figures. This could happen
partially through a decrease in the rate of inflation, and we have
succeeded pretty well at that. This is one of the stronger points of
the Netherlands—which does not have that many, by the way. For
me it reflects the reasonableness of our unions, because the minor
price increases we've had here are surely partially a consequence of
the fact that wage increases have been dealt with cautiously. In short,
I have to admit that the matter of interest rates is also of significance.
I am just a little less anxious about it than some of our colleagues
and a number of politicians.

*Are you also less anxious about refueling inflation by, I assume, a rather
forceful stimulation policy?*

Yes, I have already said that. The other objection brought up here
is that there will be new price increases, and of that I am, indeed,

afraid. Furthermore, I have mentioned two measures that could eventually, if necessary, be applied. On the one hand, at the time of recovery, we could take money out of circulation, and on the other hand, should it be necessary, we could think about an incomes policy. One of Dr. Witteveen's essays, which we discussed earlier, also pointed to the "seesaw tax" (i.e., tax rates which move in the same direction as economic indicators), which he himself implemented at the time as Minister of Finance. This means that in the current phase of the economic cycle certain taxes could temporarily be lowered somewhat. This shows that he, too, is not that concerned about the budget deficit. He seems to take the point of view, furthermore, that even a temporary increase in the budget deficit does not necessarily have to be completely rejected. On the other hand, I do want to concede to the governments and also to a number of colleagues, that we must eventually move towards a normal situation. That is to say, we must lower the budget deficit in the area of government spending. But I can only see some of that happening—in some cases almost automatically—at the moment of real recovery. If benefits decreased a little, you'd get a certain lightening in the load of expenditures, which wouldn't be harmful. There is, of course, always the tendency to vote in new expenditures. This has certainly been the case in the past, and reconsidering them from time to time, as we are doing now, can't hurt. Just to mention one well-known example: the number of advisory bodies created always has the tendency to increase, and consequently these bodies continue their separate existences, which is not always necessary. An example of the reconsideration I mentioned is the fact that we've made a list of institutions that have fulfilled their tasks and which may now be allowed to disappear. We all know examples in our own environments of things which were set up too nicely during the sixties. I even want to contend that my own university, the Erasmus University, has clearly been built in a more luxurious way than the Free University.

I should like to return for a moment to international questions, and in particular to the matter of the IMF and possible expansion of the quotas. Could this possibly run into problems because of countries that have enormous debts? Those countries already have great trouble in paying their debts and making their interest payments. I could imagine that the IMF would be very hesitant to continue expanding the quotas.

I again have to point out that monetary questions are the most difficult for me. I would, therefore, like to temper what I say because in this arena I do not have such control over the matters at hand that I could give a truly complete picture. Incidentally, these matters have been answered in Witteveen's essays, which I've just read. He himself, in a lecture honoring Per Jacobson, a well-known monetary specialist, proposed a number of new tasks for the IMF. I found myself in favor of these tasks and they renewed my impression that Witteveen—who knows his subject matter—still sees possibilities. He spoke, among other things, about a kind of insurance possibility for banks with problems that result from extending credits, and he intended this insurance possibility to come under the authority of the IMF. As I've already said, he has also clearly shown that the size of the IMF can easily be increased, and that it must be increased: the proportion that used to exist between the size of the IMF's funds and world trade at the time the IMF was founded is something we'd forgotten about. Summarizing all this I would again say: Undoubtedly there are problems here, but we can apparently also think of solutions. I was very intrigued by what Dr. Witteveen said in that lecture.

Perhaps for a moment we could take a closer look at the situation in the United States, also from the point of view of correct policy. You probably think that American policy is actually divergent from the sort of policy that Europe, in particular, would need in order to lower unemployment. Is it not so that in America we find a recovery leading to a certain decrease in unemployment?

To begin with, I'd like to contend that the recovery in the United States at the moment is clearer than in the Netherlands and even in Europe. Further, I'd like to add that, in my view, all of us in Europe are aware of the fact that at the moment Europe is in a weaker position, vis-a-vis the United States and Japan, and something certainly must be done about it. I would like to bring to mind that the

Wagner Commission, in particular, and to an extent Professor Van der Zwaan as initiator of a number of ideas from this commission, have clearly pointed out the necessity for a revitalization of our industry not simply as part of a normal economic recovery, but more in the context of a demonstrated increase of creativity in development of those industries that are capable of competing. This implicates businessmen, who apparently have not shown much imagination. I often point out that, for example, the way in which the majority of the textile industry has behaved, does not point in the direction that is now being advocated by both the Wagner Commission and Professor Van der Zwaan. To use a well-known expression, we haven't looked very hard for "new combinations"* and there are only a few companies that have escaped the difficulties our textile industry is now experiencing by doing so. There were some companies that saw this coming and set new goals in time. In my view, the most interesting example is of a Belgian firm in Ieper, which sensed years ago that the competitive position of such a labor intensive industry as textiles could not maintain its strength in Europe, and which then switched to the production of textile machines. The firm, called Picanol, has been successful with that. I know of another example in the Netherlands, the Boekelose Stoomblekerij. This small textile firm has managed to maintain its position by renovation, namely by seeking a combination of actual textile goods and plastics. I always find it helpful to give concrete examples.

Is the policy in the United States not a bit different from the stimulation policy which should be implemented here in Europe to reduce unemployment?

Indeed, it seems to me that this is presently the case. Perhaps it could be attributed to the fact that the revitalization of industry in the United States has started in Silicon Valley, where new electronic products are being made. Recently, by the way, I read that such would also be the case in other parts of America, in Massachusetts, for example. It stands as an example, then, for our direction. In addition, we ourselves have a large company, Philips, which we can expect to make a contribution in this area. It's also possible that the improvement of the situation in America is somewhat connected to

---

*J. A. Schumpeter's term.

other policies; e.g., regarding social benefits. These are extremely generous in Europe, and especially in the Netherlands, and I fear that we have to learn a lesson from this. Not as much is possible in this area as we had thought for a long time.

I want to pose a question on the issue of protectionism, because Professor Heilbroner has advocated a certain degree of it.

I just heard that from you, and it made a real impression on me. I tend not to agree with that at all. I know a number of our colleagues in England have gone in that direction—colleagues who even belong to the Labor Party. But I have to admit that I'm more convinced by the people who strongly argue against protectionism. This, of course, is correlated with the fact that I usually tend to pay a fair amount of attention to the developing countries. I believe that we should be glad in the Netherlands that this concern is generally present, and I believe we should also realize that the trouble over there is incomparably greater than here. Because of that I give priority to questions regarding developing nations when it concerns matters that are global. That means we should not be protectionistic, while, in reality, we already are. We are protectionist in the sense that, for example, we have one-sidedly stood in the path of the textile industries of certain countries. We have not only applied the so-called Multi-Fiber Agreement, but moreover, imported less from a number of countries than the amount to which they were entitled, and which had been agreed upon in negotiations for the agreement. In this regard, I find the attitude of the European Community definitely very objectionable. There is also considerable protectionism in the area of agriculture, which is damaging to the developing countries, because it would be better if world prices in the field of agriculture just now went up, so that agriculture in the developing countries themselves was stimulated. But we don't do much else than create huge surpluses and throw them on the world market; and here is where I think our policy is headed in completely the wrong direction. No matter how well I can understand that the textile industries' unions are paying attention to this matter—particularly in France, because part of the support of the socialist party comes from the North which is exactly where the French textile industry is located now—I still cannot agree with it.

Particularly in regard to those industrial sectors which in my view have no future (and that does not include the whole, but certainly a large part of the textile industry), there is only one watchword: re-education. Re-education for the industrial sectors which do have a future. There are such sectors; we have just mentioned a few, not only electronics. Aside from that I would like to point out the area of scientific research. I believe that there is a need for much more scientific research than we have presently. We already have discussed briefly that this should be coordinated in Europe. One could, of course, say: It's hard to re-educate textile workers to be scientific researchers. That is correct. We, therefore, must also provide employment possibilities in those industrial sectors for which they can be re-educated sooner. I'm thinking here not only of the metal processing industry, but also of the construction industry. I believe we can find another support for recovery here. This means renovating houses, building cheaper housing and repairing old city centers; we are doing some of that already. I am, of course, most familiar with The Hague, and there we have the Schilderswijk, a well-known, old neighborhood, but one finds similar neighborhoods in Amsterdam, Rotterdam and in other places. One thing or another is fortunately being done already, and this kind of activity is gaining popularity. I can support it strongly.

I think that Professor Heilbroner was also thinking, in particular, of Japanese competition in regard to the auto industry, and of the consequences for the United States in the form of production losses and unemployment.

I have to admit that from here I can't judge exactly if Japan herself is giving cause for that. It's very difficult to find that out. It's true they're taking steps to accommodate the pressure of the Americans and Europeans to further open their markets, but, on the other hand, there is perhaps a lack of imagination here in using those possibilities. They often say here that it is very difficult to penetrate the Japanese market. It must be, because in any case, you'll definitely have to print the instruction manuals in Japanese characters. I mean to say that we have to make the extra effort, for example, to learn Japanese. We will need a certain number of people in the business world who know Japanese. We cannot persist in the easy attitude of our Anglo-

Saxon friends, who think everyone is always prepared to learn their language. In other words, we will, indeed, have to try harder to penetrate the Japanese market, but also to do what is necessary to accomplish it. We will have to demonstrate our sales capacities. We have always been a trading nation, so here lies a special advantage for the Netherlands. We have to become more aware that Japan is a land of the future, and that we must, therefore, show a greater interest in what happens there and in what we can sell there.

So you think that Japan's strongly competitive attitude vis-a-vis the auto industry in the United States is acceptable?

Yes, it appears that the product is good, and I can hardly muster any appreciation for blocking it by means of protectionism. It has to happen through improving the quality of our product.

In conclusion:

Professor Tinbergen emphasizes the need for a coordinated and relatively expansive stimulation policy on a European and, possibly, a world-wide scale. He means—following Dr. H. J. Witteveen—that an organization such as the International Monetary Fund could really expand the availability of liquidity. Tinbergen deems the undesirability of unemployment so serious a matter that some risk pertaining to inflation can, and should, be taken. He does not see inflation becoming a danger in the near future.

Robert P. Matthews

Dr. Alan S. Blinder is the Gordon A. Rentschler Professor of Economics at Princeton. He was born in New York in 1945. He has had published a long list of books and articles of professional interest.

His article given here was written for the public of the *New York Times*.* We call it our postscript with reason. On one hand, Professor Blinder was not interviewed, as were the others, by Dr. Heertje. On the other hand, this writer and thinker was born about a decade later than the youngest of the others. Thus, it may well be that his article enhances in a different vein what major economists are today thinking about the state of the art and the problems of the coming decade.

---

*Reprinted from the *New York Times,* "Forum" of Feb. 12, 1984, page F-3, and Feb. 19, 1984, page F-3.

A KEYNESIAN REVIVAL...?

ALAN S. BLINDER

PRINCETON

For years now, I have suspected that some of my best friends have Keynesian tendencies. But pressures to conform to popular mores are strong. So most economists are too ashamed to admit it.

Oh, they often say things that sound Keynesian, all right. But if someone puts the question to them directly—"Are you of the Keynesian persuasion?"—they invariably utter a firm, if not indignant, denial. It's as if they had been accused of being a nonjogger or of hating brie.

But things are beginning to change. The Keynesians are coming out of the closet. While still shunning the label, more and more economists are uttering Keynesian code words in public. Often now I hear radical statements like "Recessions are not vacations" or "Tax cuts raise aggregate demand" coming from the mouths of economists who were previously cowed into saying the socially acceptable thing.

While this is a healthy tendency, more is needed. That's why the Committee on the Rights of Closet Keynesians (Crock) was formed in London last year.

Crock has recently issued a fascinating pamphlet, which traces how Keynesian economics fell into disrepute. Although the document is admittedly partisan, its message is worth heeding. The pamphlet makes the following points:

Within three short decades, Keynesian economics rose from being considered a dangerous abnormality to become the acceptable form of behavior for macroeconomists.

Keynesian theory was scorned at first by traditionalists who, however, had no satisfactory explanation for the worldwide depression. But stunning events have a way of breaking down dogma, and Keynesianism soon flourished in academic circles.

In 1962 John F. Kennedy became the first American President to admit publicly to being a Keynesian. And the success of his economic policies made Keynesian economics respectable. By the late 1960's, Keynesian attitudes were so prevalent that economists no more felt the need to declare their Keynesianism than to profess an interest in sex. It came naturally.

But Keynesian economics was already under attack in intellectual circles. As the pamphlet relates, the first challenge came from the monetarists.

The monetarists came out of the right, accusing the Keynesians of undermining the traditional virtues of a free-market economy, fostering inflationary expectations, and ignoring the most important economic variable in the world—M-2. (Or was it M-1?) They swept through the universities, conquered Wall Street, infiltrated the Congress, and eventually gained the upper hand at the Federal Reserve.

Crock says the success of monetarism was partly the Keynesians' own fault. A few extremists within the Keynesian community claimed that monetary policy was unimportant. To them, only fiscal policy mattered. Although the leading Keynesians rejected these views and, in fact, placed great emphasis on money, the leaders could not silence the zealots—who tarnished the image of all Keynesians.

In addition, both inflation and anti-inflation sentiment were on the rise after 1965. Monetarists labeled the Keynesians soft on inflation (which was more than half true), claimed that Keynesian economists had neither a theory of nor a cure for inflation (which was less than half true), and convinced the public that Keynesian economic policies had brought on inflation (which was slanderous).

In fact, Keynesian economics and monetarism prescribe precisely the same remedy for inflation: reduce aggregate demand and cause unemployment. It's just that Keynesians are hesitant to prescribe heavy doses of the medicine. But real monetarists don't eat quiche or shrink from recessions.

Nevertheless, blaming Keynesian policies for causing inflation is a gross misreading of history. In fact, inflation became a problem, first, because President Johnson insisted on pursuing a "guns plus butter" policy over the objections of his Keynesian advisers and, second, because natural shortages of foodstuffs and contrived shortages of oil pushed up the prices of food and energy. Yet, in a public relations coup, the monetarists managed to blame war, famine, and OPEC on the Keynesians—and to make the charges stick.

Moral: Heaven knows no fury like the wrath of an inflation-weary public.

The next attack on Keynesian economics came from a strange new doctrine that claimed to know what kind of expectations were "rational." Crock explains it this way:

Armed with space-age technology and a view that people buy and sell things at auctions held on isolated islands, the New Classical economists swept out of the Great Lakes like a winter storm, snowing the profession. The hapless Keynesians had no defense against the swift sword of Rational Expectations.

The new classicists accused Keynesians of some pretty dubious activities—like harboring Phillips curves, bearing false witness of involuntary unemployment, and assault and battery with a dead econometric model. Why did new classicism gain so many converts?

First, Keynesian economics failed to anticipate, or to prescribe a remedy for, the stagflation of the 1970's. True enough. But no one else predicted the OPEC shocks either. Nonetheless, the rational expectationists hammered away at the alleged failure of Keynesian theory, as if the theory were supposed to predict the animus of sheiks.

Second, economic theorists were charmed by rational expectations, with its appealing adjective (What was the alternative? Irrational?) and its profusion of modern mathematical and statistical techniques that made Keynesian economics look pretty prosaic. Economists hate to be called old-fashioned, so they deserted the Keynesian ship in droves.

Moral: Beware of sheiks bearing shocks.

The final assault would have made P. T. Barnum proud.

Enter the supply-siders—a well-financed but polemical bunch armed with homilies, Laffer curves, and gold bugs. They took the Keynesians by surprise—not because of anything they said, but because anyone listened.

Monetarists offered statistical evidence with no theory. New classicists offered an elegant new theory with no evidence. Combining the best of both tactics, supply-siders offered neither theory nor evidence.

Yet, with the help of an obliging mass media, supply-side economics came to be thought of as a fourth school of thought, on a par with the other three. How?

Two words seem to explain the phenomenal public relations success: politics and money. The supply-siders caught the prevailing political winds just as they shifted to the right. And their message brought music to monied ears: Government must help the rich become richer; the poor must become more self-reliant.

Moral: Never underestimate the power of an intellectually negligible idea backed by enormous sums of money.

During the past decade, the word Keynesian became a pejorative term—as in the phrase, "outmoded Keynesian idea." Advocates of monetarism, new classical economics (also called rational expectations), and supply-side economics claimed that Keynesianism had failed and deserved to be discarded like an old shoe.

Yet Keynesian economics now seems to be staging a comeback. Why this change of heart? Because events of the past decade seem to have discredited the three newer theories and verified many "old-fashioned" Keynesian ideas.

Monetarism was the first doctrine to feel the sting of reality, starting in the early 1970's.

Monetarists believe that inflation is *always and everywhere* a monetary phenomenon. But from 1972 to 1974, the rate of inflation rose while the growth of M-1 (the most basic measure of the money supply) fell. Then, from 1974 to 1976, the inflation rate fell while the money growth rate rose. Always? Everywhere?

Keynesians do not deny money a paramount role in inflation. But they stress that there are many nonmonetary causes of inflation in the short run. And they have no trouble at all explaining the rise and fall of inflation in 1972–76 by such events as wage-price controls, crop failures, and increases in the price of oil.

A central tenet of monetarism is the belief that velocity—the speed of circulation of money—behaves in a regular, predictable manner. But in the 1974–76 period velocity grew much faster than historical patterns suggested—a potentially mortal blow to monetarism.

Nonetheless, the relentless advance of monetarism in policy circles continued.

When Chairman Paul Volcker announced in 1979 that the Federal Reserve was converting to monetarism, Keynesians worried out loud that deregulation and financial innovation made velocity hard to predict, and therefore made monetarist policies hazardous. These warnings were prophetic. Velocity fell faster than anyone thought possible, rates soared, and the economy crashed.

Yet monetarism succeeded in the political arena because it was seen as a better way to fight inflation than 1960's Keynesianism. So the dramatic fall in inflation between 1980 and 1982 vindicated the monetarists. Right? Wrong. According to monetarist doctrine, you slow inflation by slowing monetary growth. But the growth rate of M-1 was the same in 1981 as in 1980 and then rose during 1982. From a monetarist perspective, this is puzzling. From a Keynesian perspective, it is easy to see what happened: High rates killed the economy.

Events have dealt even more harshly with new classical economics. But to see why, we need to know something about the theory.

According to new classical thinking, people know oodles about economics and statistical inference (that is what is meant by "rational" expectations), but have neither telephones nor newspapers to bring them the important economic data they need. They live in a competitive economy in which prices and wages dance energetically to the drumbeat of supply and demand because all goods, including labor, are sold at auction. There are no unions, no long-term contracts, and all unemployment is voluntary—maybe even optimal.

There's more. According to the theory, tight money leads to recession only if the tightening is unanticipated. Similarly, easy money brings on a boom only if it comes as a surprise. Changes in the money supply that are anticipated cause inflation or disinflation directly, without changing employment. So, in particular, an announced policy of slower monetary growth should bring down inflation without causing a recession.

These ideas are wildly at variance with events of the past decade. Did we lower inflation in 1974–76 and in 1980–82 without recession? Were the high unemployment rates of 1973–76 and 1981–83 really evidence of mass vacations? Were these recession/vacations caused by surprise changes in the money supply? The answer to each is a resounding no. And these are also the Keynesian answers.

Many Keynesians are willing to entertain the notion that expectations are rational. But they doubt that the economy is usefully thought of as an auction. Instead, they emphasize institutional features, such as labor unions and long-term contracts, that tend to insulate prices and wages from fleeting changes in supply and demand. They believe that tight money squeezes the economy whether it is anticipated or not. And they doubt that the rising unemployment that accompanies recessions is optimal, or even voluntary.

These are some of the outmoded ideas that got Keynesian economics branded as the wave of the past. Gradually, however, the force of events is showing that the new classical emperor, though resplendent in theoretical elegance, has no empirical clothes.

Ironically, it was the political success of supply-side economics that exposed its lack of intellectual foundations. We tried it, and it failed. Supply-siders claimed that, contrary to outmoded Keynesian (and monetarist) ideas, inflation could be fought from the supply side without recession. In fact, we had the worst recession since the 1930's.

They claimed that sharp reductions in marginal tax rates would get America working, saving, and investing again. Instead, working, saving, and investing all plunged—just what Keynesians say always happens in recessions.

Supply-siders claimed that tax revenues would rise to balance the budget because the gross national product would take off while the tax-avoidance industry withered away. Instead, the deficit ballooned, G.N.P. withered, and the tax-loophole industry took off.

In sum, the supply-side experiment restored faith in Keynesian economics in a way that scholarly debate never can.

Does the apparent failure of monetarism, new classicism, and supply-side economics mean that we must go back to the Keynesianism of the 1960's? Certainly not.

Each has left its mark on Keynesian economics—as have many other influences. Modern Keynesianism emphasizes the importance of monetary policy without de-emphasizing everything else. It often incorporates rational expectations as a working hypothesis, but rejects most of the rest of new classicism. Keynesians are keenly aware that the supply side of the economy can sometimes be overwhelmingly important. And we all now realize that the job of stabilizing the economy is a lot harder than we thought it was 20 years ago.

But the central tenets of Keynesianism remain much as they were 20 years ago: The private economy is not a giant auction hall, and will not regulate itself smoothly and reliably; recessions are economic maladies, not vacations; the Government has tools that can limit recessions or fight inflation, but it cannot do both at once, and neither constantly growing money supply nor constantly shrinking tax rates will cure all our ills.

It may be premature to declare the Keynesian Restoration is upon us, but someone has to say it first.

Jan Swinkels b.f.m.

Dr. Arnold Heertje is Professor of Economics at the University of Amsterdam. He was born in 1934 in Holland.

He has lectured at the universities of Antwerp, Bochum, Brussels, California at Berkeley, London, Münster, Naples, Paris, Saarbrücken, and others. Professor Heertje has been a regular writer for several Dutch journals. He has contributed to many radio and television programs on economic and social issues, and has written numerous books, several having been translated into various languages. Further, he carries advisory functions for such corporations as NCR-Nederland and Nashua Nederland.

AFTERWORD
ARNOLD HEERTJE

AMSTERDAM

The conversations with ten prominent economists presented in this book demonstrate that opinions concerning the recovery of the world economy vary widely. There are differences as to how much of a recovery is occurring, as well as the permanence of improved production and employment possibilities.

These differences of opinion cannot all be traced to diverse political points of view. Economists differ in opinion for reasons other than those of politics. It is understandable that one economist, in explaining unemployment, takes more factors into account than another. Each may also present differing views as to the significance of various causes mentioned for unemployment. This range of opinions also influences the development of the economists' views for the future. Moreover, whether one is, by nature, an optimist or a pessimist can also play a role.

Political differences are especially a factor when one asks economists which policy they think best for bringing about a recovery of investment and employment possibilities. Economists then act as citizens. Their opinions are of similar value to those of other citizens.

If Keynes were alive today he would probably suggest a more expansive policy than is actually being followed. This economic-political advice would be rooted in his theory, which determines the quantity of production and employment possibilities through expenditures. His advice, however, contains a political choice which others might reject. Even if the seriousness of unemployment is widely recognized, one can differ in opinion as to which instruments should be used to restrain and lower it. While Friedman almost exclusively depends on restraining growth of the money supply, Tinbergen and Galbraith advocate an expansive government policy. Tobin, on the other hand, wants to see the money supply expand further, while Heilbroner points to the role of technical developments.

Whoever expected the ten conversations to produce a ready-made solution for unemployment is probably disappointed. Such an expectation, however, is not justified. It is more likely that the complicated nature of the questions which one must see in a global perspective is emphasized through the diversity of opinions, all of which contain some truth. Choosing the optimum policy is, and will remain, a political matter.